The Redhead Book

A Book For And About Redheads

Al Sacharov

Word of Mouth Press

Dedicated to my dear son Russell, and wife Mary, both fellow redheads.

Illustrations by Nancy Barry
and Beth Lehnert

First printing—1,000
Second printing—3,000
Third printing—3,000
Revised edition—3,000

ISBN 0-910027-04-8
Library of Congress Number 85-51636

Additional copies may be ordered by sending
$7.95 to Word of Mouth Press, P.O. Box 824
Yonkers, NY 10701.

Have you never heard of the League of the Redheaded Men? Why, I wonder at that, for you yourself are eligible for one of the vacancies.

To Marty,
Good fortune to a swell redhead - your bro' said so!
Al Sacharov

Thanks

Sometimes "thank-you" seems so inadequate a phrase to convey the profound gratitude you feel towards a person. But since it's the best the English language has to offer, I extend a heartfelt "thank-you" to those people who have assisted me in my efforts: Sted Noble, Dr. Lendon Smith, Prof. Adell Patton, Adele Sacharov, Peter Post, David Post, Andrea Putman, Gen. A.S. Newman, Teri Bryan, Maurice Silverman, Harry Rand, the staff of the Library of Congress, Rosslyn Stevens for her lucid translations, Leo Byrne for his guidance, Maureen Malloy and Chris Straub for proofreading, Bill and Molly Mitchell for editing, Mary Feldman for indexing and her wonderful support, the folks at the Glen Echo Writer's Center for creating a writer's Nirvana, and to all redheads past, present and future who shared with me their energy to pull this book through.

I promised I wouldn't forget. . .Special thanks to my illustrators—Nancy Barry for her character sketches and Beth Lehnert for her chapter and cover designs.

Contents

Preface

Some people are born redheads, others choose to be redheads, but in either case, it's tough to ignore redheads. They simply have a way of standing out in a crowd. I know, because I am one. I really didn't have much choice in the matter. There are some physical quirks foisted upon you at birth that, for better or worse, affect your whole life. Big ears, for instance, or buck teeth, or red hair.

I used to hate having red hair, mostly because of a stupid little phrase that kids used to say (and I guess they still do) which goes, "I'd rather be dead than have red on the head." To this day I have never figured out the meaning of this poem except that dead, red and head all rhyme. Actually, my hair color is more along the lines of strawberry blonde, but nine-year-olds usually don't make such fine shades of distinction. For most of my ninth year I attempted to be less obvious by wearing a hat, but that didn't solve the problem of freckles. Freckles and fair hair have a natural affinity for one another. Mine resembled a perpetual case of measles. One of my teachers said they had to do with pigment, but I ignored her since I couldn't see the relationship to pork chops. Instead, I used to joke and say they were trying to organize themselves into a terrific tan.

Luckily, as I grew older, I became less self-conscious about the color of my hair and more self-conscious about losing it. In fact, I grew to like, even love, having red hair. I thought it looked distinguished and provided me with a certain amount of class. During this period when my outlook on hair was being improved, I was meeting other redheads and discovering they also went through the cycle of embarrassment to pride that I experienced. We idly started to compare notes about ourselves and realized we had more than hair color in common. A certain amount of feistiness, restless energy, exuberance and a willingness to take risks were qualities that I found were not mine alone.

From being a mere point of curiosity, the idea began to form in my mind that there is something special about redheads. Not that this was a unique idea, or a good idea, or a bad idea, but it certainly was a damned persistent idea. It wouldn't let go of me. I became like a pregnant woman who suddenly starts seeing other pregnant women popping up all over the place. Everywhere I turned I noticed redheads, not only in public, but in novels, portraits and films as well. Finally, with the encouragement of some wonderful friends, I decided to take a look at what it truly means to be a redhead.

My initial plan was simply to do a series of short biographies about well-known redheads, sort of a "Who's Who of Hair Color." Since I was living near Washington, D.C., I began by contacting the vast number of associations and lobbying groups headquartered in the city to see if any of their distinguished members had red hair. The answers were usually, "I'm sorry, but no department in our office is concerned with red hair," or, "By the time they get to be famous, they're either bald or gray-haired, so I really don't know." Then I combed the card files of the Library of Congress, but all that turned up was *The Red-headed League* by Arthur Conan Doyle (better known as the man who embarked Sherlock Holmes on his detective career). I was nearly ready to abandon the attempt, but the idea would not loosen its hooks. It started acquiring an energy force that sucked in the facts needed. Names of well-known redheads trickled forth, along with extraordinary material on redheads in history and religion. Mere biography and anecdote, however, no longer proved enough to satisfy my curiosity. I wanted to seek the soul of redheadedness, and in doing so I uncovered references to obscure studies that provided vital links between hair color and personality traits.

Aspects of my own behavior gradually were brought into

clear focus for the first time, and the project evolved into a fascinating journey of self-discovery. It stops somewhere short of shaking the foundations of psychology, but I nonetheless now feel that the way I perceive the world has a lot to do with my being a redhead. Redheads have historically been pioneers, innovators and adventurers; and perhaps what this planet needs is a fresh dose of that energy. If this book in any way raises the consciousness of redheads to realize the vibrancy of life that is their birthright and helps them channel that gift to inspire others, then I have succeeded in my purpose. Maybe the next generation of redheads will then be treated to the rhyme, "I'd feel dead without red on my head."

1

Hair She Comes, Hair She Grows!

I'd rather have Fingers than Toes,
I'd rather have Eyes than a Nose;
As for my Hair
I'm glad it's all there,
I'll be awfully sad when it goes!

Gelett Burgess,
Nonsense Verses

You can comb it, twist it, braid it, pull it, dye it, cut it, lose it, part it, fluff it or tease it, and hair will still be hair. No doubt about it, hair is fairly remarkable stuff. More attention has been paid to it than any other part of the visible human anatomy, and untold scores of books and magazine articles have been written about its care and adornment. A large part of this human fascination with hair is because of the striking effect it can have on others. Your hair style is a statement of your personality. It reflects how you want others to react to you on a first impression basis. You can change your clothes, but it takes a long time to change your hair. It subtly identifies you with your goals in life, your social standing and your position in the community. If you don't believe this, try recalling the last time you saw an investment banker wearing a ponytail. On a larger scale, the whole philosophy of the hippie movement centered arount the freedom associated with wearing long hair.

Styles change to reflect the times, but there are certain basic factors of hair growth common to all types and shades, irrespective of whether a person is a blonde, brunette or redhead. Technically speaking, hair is an outgrowth of the epidermis that appears on all mammals.In humans, it appears on a fetus between the sixtieth and one-hundreth day after conception. Hair appears all over the body except for the palms and soles of the feet. Its primary purpose is to insulate the head against heat loss, but to a lesser extent, it also aids in sweat absorption and perception.

A strand of hair, when viewed in cross-section through a microscope, consists of three distinct regions. The outermost layer is called the cuticle and consists of flat, overlapping cells that resemble the shingles of a roof. Although extremely small, (one micron, or one thousandth of a millimeter in thickness, and 45 microns long), the cuticle cells provide waterproofing to the two inner layers.

The second layer of the cross-section is known as the cortex. It supplies the major portion of the hair fibre and contains the pigment granules and oil pockets that endow hair with its color and sheen. The cortex cells average six microns in thickness and 100 microns in length. Their spindly shape enables the cells to twist about each other and thus give hair its body.

The innermost layer of hair is called the medulla. It is not present in all hair, especially the fine lanugo hair that covers the arms and legs. The medulla has received little scientific attention since its cells are difficult to isolate. One interesting fact, however, has been discovered. Medulla cells are known to dehydrate, thus leaving a series of small air spaces at the center of the hair.

Protein and moisture are the major components of the three hair layers. The 21 amino acids in hair protein compose 65 to 95 per cent of hair weight. Moisture content accounts for up to 32 per cent, and fatty acids total nine per cent. Trace elements make up less than one per cent of hair content, but they provide fascinating keys to a person's health. Twenty-five elements, including aluminum, calcium, selenium and gold have been isolated in hair strands. Since the hair follicle is dependent on a rich blood supply, modern medicine has been able to use trace element hair analysis to discover imbalances in the body chemistry and thus recommend corrective diets.

A Perfectly Respectable Way to Greet a Redhead

"Har, you lousy sorrel-top!"

-*My Southern Friends,* J.R. Gilmore (1863)

Hair Today, Gone Tomorrow

Hair growth begins in a tiny structure called the follicle. Imagine, if you will, poking your finger into a lump of kneaded bread dough. A long hole occurs, yet the hole is still continuous with the rest of the dough. Poke a few thousand holes in the dough and you'll get an enlarged version of how the skin looks.

Each follicle grows into the inner layer of skin, or dermis, in a slanted fashion, which accounts for the "lay" of the hair. When the pattern is harmonious, the hair is easy to part. Cowlicks occur because of follicle whorls clashing against one another.

On the sides of the slender hair follicle is a network of nerves, and a muscle named the arrectores pilorum. This muscle is part of the involuntary nervous system. When activated during times of cold or fear, it contracts and creates "goose bumps." The involuntary nerves also control the output of the sebaceous sacs surrounding each follicle. These sacs create a substance called sebum which oozes directly against the hair strand, literally greasing it as it emerges through the epidermis. The reason for the common complaint of dry hair in winter is that cold weather diminishes the sebum output.

The hair follicle attains its greatest diameter at the base, where it expands into a bulb. This is the true beginning of the hair shaft. Within the bulb are blood vessels called the dermal papilla which supply the energy and oxygen necessary for hair growth. During hair growth, cells actively divide at the base of the bulb and move to the narrower tip, where they elongate and align themselves vertically. At the tip of the bulb, the hair technically "dies" since cell division no longer occurs. Nonetheless, the hair does not harden for one-third of the way up the follicle. The interior of the follicle acts as a mold; this mold, or sheath, determines hair texture to a large extent. The sheath for straight hair is mostly circular; wavy hair is oval and kinky hair is convex. Soon after the hair cells harden, the sheath cells are digested by enzyme action.

Freed from its constraints, the hair continues up the follicle, gets lubricated by the sebaceous sacs and emerges into the light of day at the rate of .35 millimeters a day, or an inch every six weeks. Ah, but not forever. Although it can last over a long period of time, hair growth is not continuous. The follicle goes through a distinct cycle of rest, growth and transition. In the resting phase, no cell division occurs and the sides of the bulb shrink and press against the hair shaft, which has developed brush-like tufts at the base to anchor it firmly. When activity begins, the follicle elongates and a column of cells, called the vital strand, is sent downward from the aging strand and forms the nucleus for the generation of a new hair. The new hair strand forms and displaces the old hair within the follicle. The old shaft becomes loosened and is either brushed or combed away, or pulled out without effort.

Growth continues at a fairly even rate until the hair reaches its maximum length, which, if left uncut, can reach several feet. It then develops the brush-like tufts. The follicle deteriorates rapidly during the transition stage and again begins its resting cycle. Dermatologists have not yet determined what exactly triggers this cycle of generation, which can allow a human scalp hair to grow continuously for up to 20 years. However, they do feel that hormones, nutrition and a person's general state of health play a large part in the process.

From Beyond the Grave

One of the most common beliefs about hair is that it continues to grow after death. Physicians maintain that it cannot possibly do this since hair needs a blood supply to live. What usually happens is that a small additional amount of hair may be revealed due to skin shrinkage.

However, one curious case on record concerns Elizabeth Siddal, the beautiful wife of poet-painter Dante Gabriel Rossetti. When Elizabeth committed suicide in 1862, her grieving husband buried with her a sheaf of love poems. Seven years later, and in need of cash, Rossetti asked his friend, Charles Howell, to exhume her body and retrieve the poems for publication. When Howell opened the coffin he was flabbergasted. Elizabeth Siddal's golden-red hair practically filled the box. Had it grown in the grave? Nobody was certain. Perhaps Howell was exaggerating, or perhaps her hair was already that long at her death, or perhaps Elizabeth Siddal was simply a remarkable redhead.

Pigmentation Is Not A Porkchop, Or Is It?

If a redheaded girl is born, there was a pig under the bed.
-Irish proverb

The Irish certainly have a knack for conveying ideas in a whimsical fashion. For those of you with an inquiring turn of mind, this "barnyard" theory must surely bring up a few intriguing questions. Were redheaded girls only born on farms? Were the Irish lax housekeepers or did they simply love animals? What did the pig think of this idea? If you can't come up with any answers off the top of your head, then perhaps a scientific explanation will satisfy your curiosity.

Cursory examination shows that hair has a wide variety of colors, but only two chemically distinct pigment granules have been isolated—eumelanin for dark hair; and pheomelanin for light hair. The genetically controlled production of these two agents, and the densities in which they occur, bring about all the different shades of hair color in existence. The two color elements are formed by the blending of enzymes and amino acids in pigment cells called melanocytes. The key amino acid is tyrosine, which appears more profusely in dark hair than in light. We will later see that these quantity levels may have a lot to do with the relationship between hair color and behavior because of tyrosine's equally important influence on brain chemistry and brain cells.

The melanocytes lie dormant at the base of the hair follicle until it begins its phase of active growth. At that point, activity increases and pigment granules, measuring .15 microns in diameter, are formed. These granules are then gathered by the cell into tightly rounded bundles and transferred to the cortical area of the newly forming hair shaft. The granules then disperse and by the time the hair shaft leaves the scalp it has attained its true color. When hair turns gray or white, it is due to the failure of enzyme action in the melanocytes, which is at present an irreversible breakdown. For blondes and brunettes, this is the end of the story, but redheads have more going for them—one page more to be exact.

In 1945, two doctors at the University of Chicago, Peter Flesch and Stephen Rothman, experimented to see if there was indeed a special chemical quality pertaining to red hair. They appealed to barbers throughout Illinois to send them clippings of red-haired customers and, when they gathered about two and a half pounds of hair, the two researchers went to work. The hair was treated with hot acid and then filtered and allowed to dry. What remained was a purplish-red pigment that did not appear in any other hair shade of mammals. The pigment was found to be a very complex iron compound which Flesch and Rothman named trichosiderin. It appeared in only minute amounts. From 100 grams of bright red hair, 40 milligrams of trichosiderin were recovered. The dissolving out of trichosiderin did not change the color of the hair, but it did cause it to lose its lustre. Faced with this evidence, Flesch and Rothman assumed that the trichosiderin somehow modifies or oxidizes pigment granules without being changed itself. Studies by other researchers determined that trichosiderin appears in varying amounts between all the different shades of red hair. It acts as a unifying link for the various tints, including the red hair of Negroes belonging to the Yoruba, Bini and Ibo tribes of Nigeria.

How Could We Live Without Her?

Dear Ann Landers,

You really dropped your buckets when you replied to those two grandmothers who were baffled by the sudden appearance of a redheaded grandchild. How is it that you don't know that non-hereditary redheadedness is an American melting pot genetic trait?

I am sure there are others who have suffered needlessly because of suspicions in regard to their parentage. Please check with your experts and tell the grandmas it wasn't the milkman, the postman, "Miss Clairol" or rusty pipes. A redheaded baby with a blonde dad and a brunette mama is as American as apple pie.

Excerpted from the Washington *Post* on September 10, 1981

We shouldn't really be too hard on Ann, for the truth of the matter is, nobody really knows what causes red hair. It has been with mankind since the beginning of recorded history, and it no doubt existed in even earlier times. It is definitely an inherited characteristic, but its method of inheritance is still obscure since there are so many possible gene-pairings that can occur. Mice, for instance, are the most frequently studied mammal for genetic research and, in their case, at least 15 different gene-combinations determine hair pigmentation. Researchers have found it difficult to exactly match degrees of redness between parents and children since red hair tends to darken with age. Another problem with studying redheads is that red hair is not always consistent throughout the body. Persons having less than 10 per cent of their hair bright red, and the rest of a brunette shade, are common examples, as are men with dark hair and red beards. In addition, red hair is usually affected by exposure to sun and water. Women in

Renaissance times, for instance, washed their hair in sea water to create the well-known color of "titian red."

It seems fairly certain, however, that two redheaded parents will have redheaded children. In a study conducted in England, the 11 children of four pairs of red-haired parents all had red hair. Red hair appears to be a recessive tendency, as opposed to dark hair. For this reason, redheads have appeared in families that have had dark-haired members for several generations, but where, at one earlier point, redheads were present. Within the same family, if one of the parents is dark-haired and the other red-haired, it is usual to see both hair colors appear in the children. It is a matter of chance, genetics and, from the redhead's point of view, pure good fortune.

Redheads are present in all parts of the world, but most commonly they appear in Northern Europe, North America and Australia. One of the greatest concentrations of redheads lives in the Highland regions of Scotland, where nearly 11 per cent of the people have red hair. Closely following is Ireland, with around 10 per cent, and the percentages level off to nearly five per cent for other European countries such as Russia, Denmark, England and Sweden. A significant number of redheads are also found among the Jewish population, with four per cent of the ethnic group being redheaded. In the United States, redheads compose two per cent of the population, or over four million people.

By the Prophet's Beard

A popular way to apply a red tint to hair is by using henna, which is a dye made from a shrub, *lawsonia inermis,* that grows throughout the Middle East and India. The dye is prepared by shredding the leaves and twigs of the plant into powder and then stirring in hot water. The paste is applied to the hair and allowed to remain overnight to set the tint, which then lasts for several weeks. In addition to being used as a dye, henna is also thought to have magical properties. In more remote areas of Arab countries, an application of henna and coriander seed is believed to keep away malevolent spirits called the *jinn.* Special designs painted in henna are also a protection against the evil eye. Such strong spiritual belief is placed on the benefits of henna that the Prophet Mohammed is said to have dyed his beard with the substance, thus leading to the Arab affirmation, "By the Prophet's beard."

Now For A Few Words About Freckles

> I think freckles on the skin are due to some salt of iron, sunlight brings them out by reducing them from high to low states of oxidation—perhaps with a powerful magnet applied for some length of time and then with proper chemicals, these mudholes of beauty might be removed.
>
> -*The Diary of Thomas Edison*

Mudholes of beauty, indeed! I rather think they are cute, which is a mature way of viewing a situation you cannot really change. Contrary to Edison's views, a redhead can safely walk past a magnet, and not have to worry about rusting away during a rainstorm since iron is not a "freckling" factor. The common everyday variety of freckles is known to science by the name ephilides. They may occur anywhere on the body, but are most common on the face, chest, back, arms and hands. Freckles are prevalent among redheads and blondes, and they usually appear on a child around the age of seven.

Freckles, and the skin in general, are pigmented by the same melanocytes that provide hair color. Normally these cells are equally distributed throughout the dermis layer of the skin, thus allowing a person to tan evenly. But with fair-haired people, these melanocytes are concentrated in certain small areas due to genetic patterns. The larger skin area has fewer pigment cells, thus making a fair-haired person highly susceptible to sunburn. The actual pigment granules in freckles are rod-shaped, the same size as those found in people with dark skin. The other areas of the skin have spherical granules which don't react as quickly after exposure to sunlight, thus leading to sunburn. Only the ultraviolet rays of the sun stimulate the melanocytes to produce greater amounts of pigment. This is the reason freckles are more obvious during the summer than at other times of the year when the sun is less direct.

Redheads should take great care while exposing themselves to the sun. Studies have shown that prolonged doses of ultraviolet rays can induce malignant activity in pigment cells, thus leading to the dangers of skin cancer.

Changing the Natural Order of Things

How to get rid of freckles:

Freckles may be peeled off by painting the skin lightly with phenol, followed immediately by application of alcohol. Monobenzyl ether of hydroquinone may be temporarily effective.

Diseases of the Skin, George Andrews (1971)

How to get freckles:

"Sharon's secret recipe for freckle juice" — One glass makes an average amount of freckles. Mix up all these things together—stir well and drink fast. Grape juice, vinegar, mustard, mayonnaise, juice from one lemon, pepper and salt, ketchup, olive oil and a speck of onion.

P.S. The faster you drink it the faster you can get F*R*E*C*K*L*E*S

Freckle Juice, Judy Blume (1971)

2

Redheads Are Redheads Are Redheads

You could see he thought redheads
were hell on wheels.

Franklin Charles, *The*
Vice Czar Murders

A Fable

Once upon a time there was a chicken named Humphrey. Now Humphrey happened to be a Rhode Island Red who somehow got mixed in with a group of Plymouth Rocks. Nobody would cackle it out loud, but most of the other chickens felt Humphrey was definitely a bad egg. He was always crowing three hours before the sun rose and then taking off on daylong journeys to scratch for bugs and corn kernels. None of the other chickens would accompany him since they were content to stay at home, be mellow, and peck at the feed the farmer tossed them. In fact, the rest of the chickens did their best to stay clear of Humphrey. "Too intense a guy" they agreed. Well, one night Humphrey returned home from his travels only to find the coop barren except for a few stray feathers. All of the other chickens had met the chopping block because of the high demand for chicken wings as hors d'ouevres at singles bars.

MORAL OF THE STORY

"It's better to be red than dead," —or—"In a world where conformity is the norm, there are some folks who simply are different, and this difference is their gift."

The fable about Humphrey is an "eggcellent" way of illustrating the point that redheads, by their very nature, tend to be more peppy than other folks. All of my questing for the elusive quality that just sets redheads apart kept returning to one belief—the soul of redheadedness is energy—lots of energy, boundless energy, constant energy. Consider the adjectives commonly linked with hair colors—benevolent gray, tawny brown, sexy blonde—but what always goes with red—it's flaming, isn't it? Nine times out of ten there is going to be a dynamism, an electricity, an energy flow associated with a mane of blazing red hair.

At first I thought this perception was simply based on my own skimpy information. I happen to be an active sort of fellow, and so are several redheaded friends. But was this a valid sample? Were I and my friends exceptions to the rule, or did a rule exist? In other words, what about all the redheads "out there?" I was at a total loss as to quantifying this question until stumbling upon the following item in an old copy of the *Reader's Digest:*

> An Israeli researcher believes there may be some truth in the folk-wisdom in many cultures that redheaded people may be a bit temperamental. Psychiatrist Michael Bar of Israel's Shalvata Psychiatric Center reported a study showing that redheaded children are three to four times more likey than others to develop "hyperactive syndrome"—whose effects include overexcitabilty, short attention span, quick feelings of frustration and usually, excessive aggressiveness.
>
> "It is possible," he says, "that the assumed national characteristics of certain ethnic groups, like the adventurousness of the Vikings and the temperament of the Irish, are connected to the high frequency of redheads among them."
>
> -*Reader's Digest,* July, 1980

The door had been unlocked, but it still wasn't quite open. Many questions remained to be asked. Was the link-up between red hair and hyperactivity due to some biological reason or was it strictly coincidence? Where do you draw the line between hyperactive and simply active behavior? Is hyperactive behavior a blessing in disguise? The last question was a stickler, for if redheads tend to be energetic and high-strung, then these qualities are their birthright and by using their gifts they can be of great service to humanity. Dynamic energy was indeed the quality that some of history's greatest redheads used in making their mark upon the course of human events. There are, obviously, times when everyone manifests traits of intense activity or lethargy, and to say that all redheads are hyperactive is simply too broad a generalization. It would be much like remarking that all brunettes are sluggards. The whole issue appeared to revolve around the question, "If redheads are hyped up, then how hyped up?" I felt the best way to determine this outer limit of redheadedness was to understand what was meant by the term, "hyperactivity."

The Nature of the Beast

In our society, the word hyperactivity has become a buzzword for teachers, parents and pediatricians. No matter what their level of intelligence, children that are restless and overactive receive more negative reaction than does the inactive child. The story is told of Winston Churchill, a redhead, that his teachers were so exasperated by his constant motion they resorted to letting him run around the school grounds between classes to burn off excess energy. In today's schools, however, there are more deceptively easy ways to insure compliant behavior—drugs. A 1970 report observing elementary schools in Omaha, Nebraska, reported that between five and ten per cent of the grade school children were on some sort of behavior modifying drug. Since that time, a great deal of closer monitoring has taken place, but the issue of hyperactivity has not disappeared. In elementary schools alone there are estimated to be nearly five million hyperactive children.

What exactly, though, does this word mean? As the name suggests, it involves an excessive amount of activity in situations where it is clearly inappropriate.

Although each case manifests itself uniquely, symptoms include poor concentration, easy distractability, constant attention-getting activity, anti-social behavior such as stealing, learning problems due to poor memory, difficulties in coordination, aggressive behavior towards peers, immaturity, lack of discipline and low frustration-tolerance.

These words describe conditions of hyperactive behavior at its limits, and rare is the child who does not manifest a few of these qualities at some point in his life. But with hyperactive children they are more constant. Aspects of this behavior often appear early in childhood, and it becomes quite pronounced when the child enters school. In the classroom, hyperactive children are observed to fidget more, leave their seats more often, wander about the class, and in general, behave more restlessly than other children.

There are other physical disorders that can occur concurrently with the personality traits, such as food allergies, hypoglycemia, alcoholism, insomnia and migraine headaches. As might be guessed, some of these problems appear later in life, since it is unusual to find a seven-year-old with a muscatel habit. Hyperactivity, in fact, can go both ways as a person matures. Its symptoms can diminish in adolescence or later life, or an individual can carry them on into adulthood. Taken to its extremes, unchecked hyperactivity can result in psychiatric disorders such as depression or explosive tempers. On the other hand, hyperactive adults are extremely well-suited to jobs that require endless energy, an outgoing manner, physical risk, quick decisions and individual freedom.

The syndrome of hyperactivity first came to medical attention around the turn of the century. Although the condition certainly existed prior to then, the world had enough frontiers to absorb the restless urges of those folks who needed more elbow room. You didn't have to be energetic to be a pioneer, but it certainly helped. The earliest research efforts were devoted to trying to match hyperactive behavior with aspects of physical brain damage. But in the 1960s there was a shift in emphasis to a more psychological approach. Now it is felt that although brain damage may appear in certain individual cases, hyperactivity is a complex behavioral pattern, brought about by genetic and chemical influences and affected to a certain extent by the social environment.

Books have appeared contending that hyperactivity is a myth constructed by intolerant parents and teachers against normally exuberant kids, a myth that has been aided and abetted by drug companies viewing a megabuck marketplace. There is indeed a danger in viewing all rambunctious behavior as hyperactive but, to give a certain amount of credit to parents, they usually know when they have a "wild man" on their hands. Numerous tests, such as the Achenbach Child Behavior Checklist, have also been devised to help put the hyperactive syndrome on a more objective basis. These tests can help determine if a child's behavior is indeed deviant for his age.

If a child is felt to be hyperactive, and a problem to himself and others, there are several methods of treatment that are in current vogue. The use of drugs has already been mentioned. They do calm a child and enable him to concentrate, but the danger involved is that once they are phased out the child or adolescent still has to face a host of emotional and psychological problems. Behavioral modification, by effectively trained teachers and parents, is thus needed in conjunction with drug programs, to serve as a useful method of encouraging productive social behavior.

Perhaps the most intriguing new therapies involve changing dietary patterns. Doctors have reported that by eliminating food additives, white sugar and white flour from the diets of hyperactive clients, many have experienced remarkable improvement in bringing more self-control to their behavior, while at the same time decreasing troublesome allergy symptoms.

In discussing hyperactivity, a certain amount of caution is needed. Otherwise, there is the tendency to fall into the trap of the first-year medical student who, upon reading his texts, decides he has leprosy, tuberculosis and dengue fever, all affecting him simultaneously. Our poor medical student may just be suffering from a case of the blues or a common cold that colors his perception. Similarly, most cases of high-strung behavior do not cause problems unless they are truly outrageous. Think about it—if all the redheads throughout history had manifested the extremes of hyperactivity, the world would have combusted into oblivion ages ago.

The High-Octane Redhead

If redheads do have a tendency to be "wired" at a high-energy level, is this due to coincidence, heredity or environment? The interplay between these agents has challenged researchers since modern psychology became established as a discipline, and in the case of redheads there is evidence pointing towards genetic and biological linkups that affect behavior.

Dr. Bar (of *Reader's Digest* fame) published the full results of his study in a paper entitled *Hyperactive Behavior in Redheaded Children.*

"In the past," he wrote, "red hair has been connected in folk beliefs to hyperactive-aggressive behavior. The first description of the hyperactive syndrome is illustrated with redheaded children. Figures with red hair appear in the Bible. Esau, for example, was described as an impulsive hunter. Since red hair is an inherited factor, probably transmitted as a recessive gene, positive evidence for a connection with the hyperactive syndrome would strenthen the hypothesis of a genetic factor as one of the causes for the hyperactive syndrome. The hypothesis was therefore examined showing that the frequency of redheaded children is higher among hyperactive children than among the general population of children"

Dr. Bar and his colleagues selected 45 redheaded school children (aged 6-12), with hair shades ranging from strawberry blonde to auburn as a test group, and a slightly larger number of dark-haired students as a control group. Both parents and teachers filled out behavioral questionnaires concerning the children, and when the results were tabulated, both parents and teachers rated the redheads as being higher in hyperactive behavior, especially among the boys. Dr. Bar noticed that, "In the hyperactive group, more than two-thirds were redheads. In the non-hyperactive group, more than three-fourths were from the control group, a very pronounced difference.

"It is generally accepted that people are born with constitutional factors affecting activity levels and, in a continuum of activity, the more active children, and this is decided arbitrarily, are called hyperactive. The cause of hyperactivity may be constitutional or genetic, or due to the influence of the child's environment. For most children it is a mixture of the two. The present research appears to have identified an association between the inherited factor of red hair and the level of activity in children in regular elementary schools. It therefore provides evidence to support the hypothesis of a genetic element in hyperactivity. The children chosen for this research come from ordinary schools and not from psychiatric clinics. This means that the children were not from the extremes of the activity continuum, and they were not very different from other children."

Dr. Bar brought up two very important points in his article.The first was that the levels of hyperactivity are arbitrarily chosen. In a warrior-society a great amount of energy and impulsive behavior would be viewed as essential for survival, where the same energy in present society, is a liability when a person is forced to stay desk-bound all day in school or at work.

Secondly, he emphasized the importance of genetic transmission and its link with red hair. Current research is indicating that hyperactivity is most likely the result of an inborn temperamental difference in the child. How the child is treated and raised can affect the severity of the problem, but it is doubtful if this causes hyperactivity.

This leaves us with the question of what in the gene structure brings about this behavior, and how it relates to red hair. A Portland, Oregon, researcher, Dr. Lendon Smith, is advancing the theory that one cause for hyperactive, or high-strung behavior, relates to the amino acid, tyrosine. In nearly 20 years of clinical pediatrics, Dr. Smith has noticed that nearly 75 per cent of the nearly 8,000 children referred to him for hyperactive behavior were fair-complected, with either blonde or red hair.

Tyrosine, if you remember, is the genetically regulated amino acid that controls pigmentation. It is also an important building block for brain chemical neuro-transmitters such as norepinephrine and epinephrine. These neuro-transmitters act as chemical gate-attendants between nerve cells. They allow the flow of electric impulses from the brain to go throughout the nervous system. When there is little pigmentation, more tyrosine is thought to be directed to the production of neuro-transmitters, thereby "hyping up" fair-haired children. This theory of Dr. Smith has several interesting ramifications. The first concerns the tendency of fair hair to darken with age, and thus, as more tyrosine is directed towards pigmentation, hyperactivity may progressively fade, as has been noticed in clinical studies. Secondly, tyrosine is also an important factor in the ability of the body to regulate its glucose levels. This may explain why certain diets seem to benefit the behavior of hyperactive people. In any case, the idea of a physiological basis for behavior is gaining increasing acceptance among the scientific community, and is a frontier of research for those psychologists studying how people respond to stress and chemical stimulation.

The Cosmic Redhead

Peter Demianovitch Ouspensky was a highly regarded mystic and occultist who, in the course of his life (1887-1947), sought to unify mysticism, religion and science. An area to which he devoted his attention was the relationship between human body types and astrological influences. The body, according to Ouspensky, was designed to serve as a receptacle for planetary forces that manifest themselves through the human being's endocrine gland system. Each person reflects the characteristics of a particular planet. Ouspensky determined that people with red hair are governed by energy from the planet Mars. Martial types are said to be courageous, vigorous and extroverted, and tend to function well in sports, the military and business. By becoming familiar with the planetary types, his students were thus able to gain greater control in understanding their social environment. Ouspensky's teachings are still being followed by groups within the United States and Europe.

To Pursue Greater Glory

The tendency for redheads to be viewed as active types has several historical precedents. In earlier days, when people were more tribal in nature, racial and physical characteristics were often uniform throughout the group. In fact, such features were often ways various cultures used to distinguish themselves from other tribes.

The references made by ancient historians to redheaded peoples usually pointed out adventuresome or aggressive tendencies. For instance, the Roman historian Pliny, who wrote from 50-80 A.D., mentioned the essential role the Seres played in conducting the silk trade between Europe and China. "The Seres," he wrote, "are of more than average height; they have red hair, blue eyes and harsh voices, and have no language in which to communicate their thoughts." Being a Roman, a certain amount of inherent egotism may be attributed to the last statement, since Pliny probably meant they did not speak Latin. The Seres served as middlemen in the silk trade, and transported the cloth on the long, arduous caravan routes that transversed Central Asia. As a trading people, they were constantly on the go. They had to cope with disasters such as landslides and ambushes that certainly added excitement to their lives. When the silk reached Rome it was worth its weight in gold, and the Romans, who had no idea of its true origin in China, referred to it as "Seric cloth."

Other redheaded tribes of Central Asia chose to be warriors instead of traders. The Turfanese people, who were described by Chinese historians as "blue-eyed and red-haired," waged nearly continual warfare against the Chinese around 100 B.C. Although eventually conquered, they were never entirely subdued and served as a thorn in the side of the Western Chinese empire.

A related group, the Epthalites, came to prominence around 400 A.D., and for the next 150 years fought throughout large sections of Central Asia, Persia and India. In one battle against the Persians, an Epthalite king had a large trench dug near the frontiers of his kingdom through which the Persian armies would have to pass. The trench was filled with water and covered by floating reeds. Only a narrow path was left intact, and when a small group of cavalry attacked the advancing Persians, they escaped over the secret passage. Not knowing about the ruse, the Persians charged full force, fell into the ditch, and those not drowned were slaughtered. The constant fighting, however, weakened the Epthalites and they were eventually absorbed into other population groups.

In Western Europe, the appearance around 900 A.D. of grim-prowed Viking ships, filled with fair-haired, bearded warriors, struck terror into the hearts of people living in coastal villages and towns. Such was their fearful impact that the faithful filled medieval churches to chant the prayer, *A furore Normannorum, livera nos Domine*—"From the fury of the Northmen, O Lord, deliver us." In addition to their exploits as pillagers and plunderers, not to mention rapists, the Vikings were also fearless explorers and traders. They reached the shores of North America to the West, and Arabia and Constantinople to the East, where one Arab contemporary, Iban Fadlan, described them as "tall as date-palms, and all red-haired."

Scores of books have been written about the effect the Vikings had on Western Europe. Their appearance in history coincided with growing population pressures in Scandinavia, and the breakdown of centralized governments, such as the Empire of Charlemagne, into tiny feudal fiefdoms. Because of their boldness and daring, the Vikings moved into this power vacuum through raiding expeditions and colonization efforts. The Vikings established many outposts in the British Isles. The history of one, centered around Dublin, illustrates how the Vikings blended their racial and cultural characteristics with the local people. In 1014, Sigtryggr "Silkbeard," the King of Dublin, was defeated by Brian Boru, High King of Ireland (and a redhead), at the Battle of Clontarf. Although they were beaten, the Vikings were allowed to remain in Ireland and eventually were assimilated into the general population. King Sigtryggr even accepted Christianity and made a pilgrimage to Rome. In England itself, the Norman conquest in 1066 was accomplished by William the Conqueror, another redhead, who was the descendent of Danish Vikings who settled in France.

It was in the East, however, that the Vikings' true ability in trade asserted itself. The riches of Arabia and Cathay tantalized their leaders, and they set out from their Baltic homes down the Volga and Dneiper Rivers to reach the wealthy city of Constantinople. The word "Russia," in fact, is thought to stem from the Scandinavian word "ruotsi" meaning "the rowing road," in reference to these river routes. Along the way, the Vikings set up trading centers that were the basis of the modern cities of Kiev and

Novrogod. Other Vikings went even further afield and crossed the Caspian Sea to reach Baghdad, a distance of over 1,900 miles. One of the Eastern wares, incidentally, which most caught their attention was silk. Over the course of time, the Vikings assimilated with the indigenous Slavs and thus added their bloodlines to Eastern as well as Western Europe. In essence, the essential roving and combative spirit of the Vikings can be summed up by the tribute paid to the Danish King of England, Knut the Great—"A King is for Glory, not for long life."

The Vikings, and the other predominantly red-haired cultures, may have had a greater influence on the course of human events than the establishment of trade patterns or the bashing of a few kingdoms. The theory could be advanced that tendencies of brain chemistry influenced the behavior of groups of people who, for reasons of warfare or trade, or both, migrated throughout the Eurasian land mass and who, by dint of their contribution to indigenous gene pools, greatly molded the character of cultures and nations that exist to this very day.

Fanciful Folklore About Redheads

There never was a saint with red hair.

Persons with red hair are usually very affectionate.

Straight, coarse red hair shows dishonesty in a person.

A lady with long, red hair is glib, talkative and vain. Her promises are seldom to be depended upon.

He is false by nature that has a black head and a red beard.

From a black-haired man keep your wife; with a red-haired man beware your knife.

In Australia, redheads are called "blueys."

Red hair denotes a person of sharp wit, unforgiving, but once a friend, a true one.

3

Redheads and Religion

The reddish, waving, abundant hair resembles the sun gods, nearly all of them being represented with an abundance of long, waving, red or yellow hair, denoting the rays of the sun.

Sarah Titcomb, *Aryan Sun Myths The Origin of Religions*

Imagine, if you will, that it is one million years B.C. No, not the movie version with Raquel Welch, but literally, in the dim ages of prehistory. Things are going just swell for you. There are plenty of mastodons to hunt and berries to pick and, although it may be your primitive imagination, it seems as if Grunta in the neighboring cave has been making eyes at you. While you are sitting on a rock contemplating whether to lovingly drag her off by the hair, an event occurs which totally freaks you out of your bearskins—an eclipse.

Where did the sun go? It was just here! Fortunately, before you reach a state of catatonic shock, the eclipse ends and the world returns to normal. The experience, however, has totally changed your outlook on life. Instead of worrying just about Grunta, you begin to concern yourself with the unseen forces controlling your physical environment—the rivers, the trees, the animals, but most of all the sun. For without the sun, nothing else would be possible. If it were to leave for good, things would be in caveman lingo-*kaput*.

The eclipse sort of shook your confidence in the old sun, and you start wondering where it goes each night when it drops behind the distant mountains. There must be a reason for its actions. Does it get tired? Hungry? Was an emergency trip to the cosmic medicine man the reason for the eclipse? As your mind starts pondering these points, you notice similarities to the sun in your own life. You, too, need rest each night and have to travel far distances. Gradually, a story takes shape that makes sense because it corresponds to both the sun's patterns and your experiences. It thus provides you with an assurance that life is proceeding on a regular, rhythmic basis. From this womb of speculation, the age of myth is born.

As man progressed, these solar myths were elaborated upon until they reached levels of high artistic beauty. They also began dealing with the deeper questions of human experience. The sun-gods were personified as mighty heroes, representing man's soul blazing across the heavens in life, to be followed by the nightly world of death and shadows, only to be resurrected in the dawn of an afterlife.

In nearly all ancient cultures, the sun myths were the focal points of religious cosmology. Since they dealt with such basic questions, it was important for the common people to visualize these myths in symbols they could understand. Hair color was highly significant, for what could be more logical than for the fiery rays of the sun to be associated with the radiant glow of red hair? In other words, as long as there has been human wonder as to origins and causes, there has been the suspicion that red hair might be part of the bridge to the supernatural and divine. The important role that redheads played in ancient religions was not limited to a single culture, but instead turned up among people separated by vast distances of time and space. Whether at one point the solar myths all had a common origin is an intriguing question, one that has occupied the attention of theologians, anthropologists and day-dreamers on a quiet, sunlit afternoon.

Statues That Fly and the Redheaded Birdman

For eons the brooding eyes of the huge stone statues looked over the vastness of the Pacific. They silently followed the flight of the sea birds, the wanderings of whales, and the rise and fall of countless tides. All that they saw they remembered. It did not matter what hour of the day it was, for darkness did not dim their sight. Theirs was a constant watch over the little island and all that passed in front of it. But never had the statues seen a sight such as this!

On the horizon were three white sails. The islanders saw the sails too, and they raced to the beach, anxiously asking each other who were these strange people approaching in mighty canoes larger than a dozen of their own? Soon the men on the ship would be asking the same question. For they were to become the first Europeans to encounter the perplexing enigma of Easter Island.

Dutch Admiral Jacob Roggeveen first sighted the island on April 5, 1722, Easter Sunday, hence its name. He had originally set out to find the mythical land of Australia and claim its riches for the Dutch West India Company. Curiosity, and a need for fresh water and supplies, prompted him to put ashore on this solitary, uncharted island. Little did he expect to find massive stone heads dotting the island, some of which were standing as tall as a ship's mast. The mysterious heads totally flabbergasted the Dutchman. "We were amazed at these stone figures," Roggeveen wrote, "because we could not understand how a people that did not have hard, stout timber could have raised them, to say nothing of the strong ropes needed to build the hoists necessary to raise the statues, some of which were a good 30 feet high and wide in proportion."

As Roggeveen left Easter Island, the natives watched as the sails passed below the horizon. The statues watched too. Admiral Roggeveen would never reach Australia, and a generation would pass before the stone eyes would again see the sun-bleached whiteness of canvas sails.

Next was the expedition of Captain Felipe Gonzales, who claimed the island for Spain in 1770. Gonzales spent over a week on the island and noted in his log descriptions of both the stones and the natives. The latter bewildered him just as much as the statues. "Their physiognomy," he wrote, "in no way reminds one of the continental Indians of Chile, Peru or New Spain. The color of their skin varies from white through swarthy to reddish. They are tall, well-built and of good proportions. Only some have black hair; that of others has a reddish or cinnamon tinge."

A remote island, populated by red-haired natives who lived in grass cottages, yet who carved 30-foot-high stone statues—to say the least, it posed a puzzle. Even in the best of conditions, anthropologists would need years to unravel mysteries the magnitude of Easter Island. But the best of conditions were not to exist. By the latter half of the 19th century, slave traders had shipped off many of the islanders to the Peruvian guano pits, while missionaries had destroyed nearly all of the sacred tablets with their hieroglyphic script. The few scraps of legend that survive tell about a mysterious energy force called *mana,* human sacrifice and a solar ceremony of spiritual death and rebirth.

Before the legends can be understood, one must consider the statues, which the natives called the *moai.* Captain Gonzales said the heads were carved as a whole unit out of rock so hard that sparks flew when he struck the moai with a pick axe. 'The carvings," he wrote, "are very rough. The only features of the face are simple cavities for the eyes, the nostrils are only just indicated, but the lips run from ear to ear in a horizontal groove. There is a certain resemblance to a neck, but no hands or feet. The section of the head covering is considerably larger than the head on which it rests, the lower edge protruding well beyond the forehead, which insures that it does not fall. This arrangement insures that the crown rests firmly on the head and prevents it from falling."

The crown which Captain Gonzales referred to was chipped out of red tufa lava. It measured six feet in height, seven feet in diameter, and was calculated to weigh 11 tons. As for the statues themselves, several hundred were carved with their average weight being nearly 40 tons. They were somehow lifted out of a 500-foot-deep volcanic crater and transported four to 10 miles to their final sites.

One theory claims they were moved via winches and rollers, but Roggeveen saw no rope or trees possible to use in this task. One difficulty with this idea is that nobody has explained the engineering needed to position the red topknots.

Some of the smaller statues were located throughout the island and on the beaches. But the most important were the ones placed on massive stone platforms of tightly fitted rock, which were called the *ahu.* As one observer wrote in 1870. "The statues. There are two kinds, there are those of the beaches which have been thrown down and broken. And there are the others, the terrifying ones, of a different spirit, that still stand a great way off, away on the other side of the island, at the far end of a wilderness where nobody goes any more."

These were the moai of power. On their heads sat the red tufa crowns and in their souls dwelt the mystery of mana. To the natives of Easter Island, mana meant the unseen energy-force that permeated the world. It was much like electricity in that it could be harnessed and directed, but never totally destroyed. When a priest or king became charged with mana, he could exert tremendous influence over nature, such as changing the weather, assuring bountiful crops or moving 40-ton statues.

Nineteenth century explorers on Easter Island noted the natives total acceptance of the mana power. Explorer Katherine Routeledge reported, "The natives never had any doubt that the statues were moved by supernatural power. We were inspecting an ahu built on a natural eminence, one side was a sheer cliff, the other was a slope of 29 feet, as steep as a house roof. Near the top a statue was lying. The most intelligent of our guides turned to me significantly, 'Do you mean to tell me,' he asked, 'that was not done by Mana?'" On another occasion, when asked how the statues were moved, one native said, "King Tiikoihu, the great magician, used to move them with the words of his mouth." Some natives claimed that on certain nights of the year the statues themselves would speak.

There can be no doubt that the priests and kings who directed 40-ton statues to transport themselves several miles were imposing figues. From where, it may be asked, did they draw their mana? Mana was thought to originate from the sun and reside in nature, since all life depended on the sun's power. In particular, the natives believed mana to be concentrated in a person's head. It was logical to assume that those persons who resembled the sun were huge storehouses of mana. This close association between the sun and a red head formed the basis for a strange religious ceremony without parallel in the whole of Polynesia—the Cult of the Redheaded Birdman.

The ceremony was held each spring to welcome the return of the sun god, Maki-Maki. In ancient cultures, the egg was the symbol of the reborn spring, and the Easter Islanders held that the egg of the sooty tern was specially significant, since the bird lived within the crater of the Mataveri Volcano, home of the moai.

In July, the spring season in the southern hemisphere, the people gathered at the foot of Mataveri. The priests would strip naked and swim across a dangerous inlet of water to the small island where the birds laid their eggs. They would chant and pray for the blessing of being the first to find an egg. The one who did find it ran to the top of the island's peak while the people cried out, "shave your head, you have the egg!" The victorious priest then shaved his head with an obsidian razor and, to symbolize the new fire of the spring sun, he painted his skull red.

He returned to Mataveri to mount the ahu near the volcano and stand among the red-crowned moai. In the eyes of the people, he became transfigured into the role of a god-man. Great feasts were held, and human beings were sacrificed at the feet of the moai. Following the festival, the god-man retired to the cliffs above the moai and lived alone until the next spring. He was the keeper of the mana for a year, a year to which he gave a dream-inspired name.

It was important for him to stay alone, for the mana that he possessed made him a high-voltage living power plant.

Any contact with lesser mortals would result in their being shocked to death. Mana was not to be treated lightly. If used improperly, the god-man could provoke earthquakes and volcanoes as easily as beneficial rains and gentle seas. The red-capped moai served as storage batteries for the god-man's mana, for the remains of the human sacrifices were buried within the ahu on which they rested. Through secret ceremonies and rituals, the god-man could tap into and wield this mana power to alter the forces of nature.

Was mana just an ignorant belief among superstitious natives? Perhaps, but it makes just as much sense as any other attempt to explain why and how the moai were carved by a people who did not even know about the wheel. However, this attempt at answering the riddle of the moai only opens the door to a roomful of other questions. Who were these Easter Islanders? Where did they come from? What happened to the mana?

No one, least of all the present-day Easter Islanders, can say for certain. Faint answers can only be interpreted from distant, half-forgotten legends. It is said that when the "child-king," Gregorio, died in the early 19th century, the sacred turtles of the Polynesians left the island, never to return, carrying away with them forever the magical force of mana. As to the origins of the islanders, legend tells of the great Polynesian sea-king, Anua-Motua, arriving to settle the island sometime around the 11th century A.D. But even at this early date, stories tell of men with pure yellow hair and huge ears already living on the island. Perhaps these early Polynesian seafarers reached Easter island and intermarried with a group of people already there, a culture so ancient that no record exists of their ever having lived, no record that is, except for the stone-faced moai watching the rising and setting of the sun.

The Relic of a God

On the South Pacific Island of Mala, the natives had a legend about a redheaded warrior-god, Sina Kwao, who visited their island ages ago. What makes this story so interesting is the relic they had of his visit. Explorer Walter Ivens wrote, in 1930, about visiting a tribal medicine man, Sulu Vuo, who had a lock of Sina Kwao's hair.

"Naturally I was amazed," he wrote, "when I first heard of this, and at once I put the obvious question to him: 'Do you mean hair that is actually red, or hair that has been reddened by the use of lime?' The answer was perfectly clear: 'Red Hair, *ifu kekora!* Hair that is colored by lime we call white, *kwao.*'"

Ivens added that the lock of red hair was kept in a wooden case and referred to as *aarai ia'ai* (The God in the Case). It was tabu for common people to see the hair or to pass in front of the case while wearing anything red.

Another South Pacific culture which puts great emphasis on red hair, is the Maori of New Zealand. A proverb among the tribe maintains, "Red hair, Chief's hair."

Redheads on the Nile

Egypt. A land so modern as to appear almost daily in newspapers, yet so ancient that on the shores of its richly-fertile Nile delta, the dawning rays of civilization dispersed the darkness of prehistory. Egypt was the light of the ancient world, an important center of culture, science and religion. Its architects built the pyramids, and its priests meditated upon the secrets of the cosmos. In reviewing our knowledge about the early Egyptians, scholar Henri Rouet concluded, "Whatever may be the case in other mythologies, I look upon the sunrise and sunset, on the daily return of day and night, on the battle between light and darkness, on the whole solar drama in all its details that is acted every day, every month and every year in heaven and earth as the principal subject of Egyptian mythology."

As this solar mythology developed, few gods were more important than Osiris. He became an all-purpose god who ruled the sun, fertility and the afterworld. Such an eminent god required a fitting sacrifice, a sacrifice that would embody his fiery splendor. Redheads filled this role, and hundreds of them would meet their end in doing homage to this powerful god of life and death.

Osiris means "many-eyed" and indicates the rays of the sun which see all parts of the earth. Originally, the god Ra represented the sun, but he was shuffled aside in a power play by the priests of Osiris, who then co-opted all of Ra's attributes for their own god.

According to Egyptian myth, Osiris was a god made man who first settled in Egypt, where he showed the people the beauties of civilization, such as agriculture and religion. Once they became proficient, Osiris left to travel over the whole earth and share his blessings with all mankind. The Egyptians, however, held a special place in his heart and he promised to return to them one day.

But while he was gone, trouble started to brew when his brother, Set, the god of darkness, grew jealous of Osiris and plotted his murder. Upon Osiris' return, Set cunningly tricked him into lying inside a box, which he then nailed shut and sealed with molten lead.

Set flung the box into the Nile and it floated far out to sea, finally landing on the western shores of the Mediterranean Sea. Meanwhile, the earth goddess, Isis, went searching far and wide for her husband's remains. After several adventures she found the body and hid it, but Set discovered the hiding place, cut the body into 14 pieces, and scattered them throughout Egypt. Because of her deep love, Isis once again recovered the parts and restored Osiris, who then became ruler of the realms of the dead. Isis and Osiris were so overjoyed to be with each other they made love and conceived the child, Horus, who had the head of a hawk and the body of a man. Although Osiris remained the lord of the underworld, he flew upwards with his son at dawn to become with him a composite god of the rising sun.

Egyptians thought so highly of Osiris because they saw in his saga the pledge of everlasting life beyond the grave. His tale is the classic solar myth of the sun bringing forth abundance, retreating into the darkness of night when its energy is scattered, and once again being reborn to rise to the heavens. It explains not only the progression of day and night, but also how the Egyptians viewed the passage of the soul into the realm of spirit.

Osirian festivals were the high points of Egyptian religious life. They were usually held in November, the month when the Nile waters receded and the fields were planted. Much wild singing and dancing took place to commemorate the joy of life before death. In homes, lamps were kept lit all night to remember the soon-to-be resurrected Osiris and the dead in general. Adding to the pageantry was the worship of the golden cow of Isis, a fertility symbol which held between its horns the sun disk of Osiris. Toward the end of this joyous period, prayers and human sacrifices were offered to Osiris;the sacrifices most favored being those of redheads.

The ancient Greek historian, Manetho, stated that Egyptian pharoahs burned red-haired men and scattered their ashes with winnowing fans. However, this may have been only one type of sacrifice, for other Greek historians suggest that redheads were beheaded. In either case, it was too bad for redheads. But it must be remembered that the Egyptians were not a brutal, barbaric people. If a human sacrifice was offered, it would have to be for a powerful reason. An early authority on mythology, Sir James Frazer, felt that burning redheads had something to do with promoting crop growth through sympathetic magic. He wrote in his classic book, *The Golden Bough:*

> The red hair of these unfortunates was probably significant. For in Egypt the oxen which were sacrificed also had to be red; a single black or white hair on the beast would have disqualified it for the sacrifice. If, as I conjecture, these human sacrifices were intended to promote the growth of crops, and the winnowing of ashes seems to support this view, red-haired victims were perhaps selected as best fitted to personate the spirit of the ruddy grain. For, when a god is represented by a living person, it is natural that the human representative should be chosen on the grounds of his supposed resemblance to the divine original.

Luckily for redheads, the Egyptians did not cultivate carrots and thus require another, oh so obvious, sacrifice. If the burning of redheads was important for agricultural purposes, then the beheading also has an intriguing significance. To the Egyptians, the head was a sacred symbol of strength and power. There are many temple paintings showing pharoahs beheading prisoners captured in battle so as to add their warlike abilities to their own. This association between the head and strength was especially important for Osirian worship. The City of Abydos, which was dedicated to Osiris, had as its seal the head of Osiris, topped by two white plumes, symbolizing the energy arising from it.

Redheads . . . Sacrifices to a sun-god . . . Belief in energy contained in the head . . . There certainly are some peculiar similarities to the previous section on the Easter Island culture. The nagging question arises, did the Egyptians also know about the mana force? Were human sacrifices made to insure crop growth by releasing the mysterious forces of nature? Present day scholar Florice Tanner writes, "They (the Egyptians) realized that life depended on an invisible energy, both in man and in the Universe. . . The Egyptians had great knowledge of natural laws, and their 'magic' was knowledge of superphysical laws. They believed in both visible and invisible powers at work in Nature."

Although it would be stretching the imagination to suggest that the Egyptians knew about the Easter Islanders on a first-hand basis, perhaps the idea of mana was a concept shared by ancient peoples throughout the world. This would certainly throw a new, intriguing light onto the riddle of how the Pyramids of Giza were constructed.

However, the definite truth as to whether the Egyptians sacrificed redheads to a sun-god to promote crop growth or to release a powerful source of energy may never be known. The answers to this question and other mysteries of ancient Egypt are lost in the sands of time. They can only be guessed at, and that is perhaps the reason the Sphinx smiles.

Was It a Coincidence?

The reign of Queen Victoria brought about colonial expansion to the point where "The sun never set on the British Empire." Ironically, the very same sun played a key role in the British conquest of Western Kenya. At the end of the 19th century, the Luo tribe, near Lake Victoria, numbered nearly a half-million members. Primarily a pastoral people, they had a sophisticated system of law, education and religion. The latter put great emphasis on prophecy, and a key prophecy told of the coming of the "red men from the sea" to whom they should show cordiality and respect. The Luo had little contact with Europeans until British official C.W. Hobley pushed into the area about 1895 to claim the land for the Crown. The Luo acquiesced to British rule instead of bitterly fighting it as did neighboring tribes. The reason for the peaceful takeover? Accompanying Hobley was a contingent of red-haired Scots and Irishmen who, after being sunburned by the equatorial sun, certainly fulfilled the description of "red men from the sea" that figured in Luo legend.

Cuchullain and Christ

Sun worship was not a totally bloody affair. The legendary heroes who came to represent the sun were the subjects of great sagas which the bards of antiquity embellished with poetic imagination and color. These narratives composed an oral tradition that served to both entertain and unite different tribes and clans of the same ethnic group. Later, as culture progressed, these stories formed the basis of written literature.

In the present day, sun-god sagas are not at all associated with the deep religious feelings they evoked. They are regarded merely as quaint stories, but this was not always the case. As Christianity began to spread across Western Europe, its missionaries encountered deep-seated forms of sun worship and religious mythology. People were not willing to part with their pagan gods, who had comforted them for generations. So the early Catholic missionaries were often forced into following the advice, "If you can't beat them, join them." The teachings and stories about Jesus Christ were thus skillfully grafted onto the attributes of the existing sun-gods. This served to make the new religion of Christianity palatable with the existing legends.

One of the most successful examples of this blending occurred in Ireland. It was through the efforts of the early Irish monks that exploits surrounding the redheaded solar-god, Cuchullain (pronounced COO-coo-lane and spelled various ways), have been recorded and saved to become a treasure chest of heroics for later generations of readers to enjoy.

Eleanor Hull, who wrote the authoritative *The Cuchullain Saga in Irish Literature,* said of the monks recording these stories,"they felt it their duty to preserve and transmit with equal care, not only the historical and geneological records of their native country, but also the great body of pagan romance they heard recited and sung around them."

In pre-Christian Ireland, the sun was worshipped under 40 different names, with that of Cuchullain being one of the most popular. Stories surrounding his life appear in 96 separate sagas, but there is such an intertwining of events and characters among the different episodes that, for the bards, it must have been presented as a connected whole.

The stories describe his hair color as changing to correspond to the time of the day. The main book of the epic, the *Tain Bo Culaigne,* pictures him by saying, "Three crowns of hair he had; next his skin, brown; in the middle, crimson; that outside formed, as it were, a diadem of gold, for like the shining of yellow gold was each glittering,curling, beauty-colored thread as free and loose as it fell down and hung between his shoulders." In the dying sun of the evening, the hair color again became red, "about his head, his hair became tangled as if it had been the branches of a red thorn-bush stuffed into a strongly fenced gap."

The tales about Cuchullain relied quite heavily on the hair image to picture the hero. They went on to describe many great qualities he possessed and adventures he encountered. For instance, so intense was the heat of his body that it melted snow 30 feet away. In the story of how Cuchullain got his name, bards told about a blacksmith named Culain who desired to entertain the Irish King, Conor, and his knights. On the day of the celebration, Culain warned the king to arrive at his house early, for each night he set loose a ferocious hound to protect his property. "He is furious with all but me," the smith said. "He has the strength and savage force of a hundred ordinary watchdogs."

King Conor and his knights arrived while there was still light in the sky, but soon they were filled with horror when the dog began to growl. The king's foster son was not with them!

The small boy had to finish his duties at the castle before he could attend the banquet, and when he arrived on the scene, the wild dog charged him. In an instant the lad grabbed the hound and strangled it. The king and Culain rushed out and saw the boy standing over the dead mastiff. Although he was glad to see the king's foster son alive, Culain was sorry his watchdog had been killed. "Fear not," said the boy, "I myself will be your hound for defence of your cattle and land." From that day on, he was called Cu-Chullain, or the "Hound of Culain," and the king's magician said to him, "One day the name of Cuchullain will ring in all men's mouths; among the brave ones of the world Cuchullain's name will find a place. Renowned and famous shall he be, beloved and feared by all."

These wonderful tales, however, began to experience competitive pressure from Christian teachings. Had the bards not adapted to the changing times, the stories of Cuchullain would gradually have faded away into forgotten lore. But with Cuchullain a smooth adaptation occurred. Because of his popularity, the storytellers began to treat him as both a contemporary of Jesus Christ and a close friend of St. Patrick. This interplay is quite evident in the following excerpt from *The Phantom Chariot of Cuchullain:*

> St. Patrick went to Tara to again preach the word of God to the King of Erin, that is upon Laegaire, son of Niall; for he would not believe in the Lord though He had been preached unto him.
>
> Laegaire said to Patrick, "By no man will I believe in thee, nor yet in God, until thou shalt call up Cuchullain in all his dignity, as he is recorded in the old stories, that I may see him, and that I may address him in my presence here; after that I will believe in thee."
>
> "Even this thing is possible for God," said Patrick.

In both spirit and action, this redheaded sun-god adapted to the coming of Christianity. One can imagine the drinkers in mead halls roaring with laughter and listening with awe while bards recited his exploits to the soft, background music of the harp. He lit the halls of winter with his bright deeds, and spread the warmth of summer with his bright rays. Perhaps it's because of their love for this former sun-god that Irishmen of today believe redheads are blessed with good fortune.

The Original Rocker and Roller

Thor, the mighty Norse god of thunder, was a boisterous, temperamental redhead who hurled a magical hammer against the evil forces of destruction threatening both gods and men. In the Norse pantheon, he was the god linking heaven and earth, and was said to rule both the weather and crop growth. From his name the word "Thursday" is derived. The early Vikings believed thunder would rumble whenever Thor traveled across the sky in his goat-drawn wagon. When he tossed his hammer at some far-off giant or troll, it would always speedily return to his right hand. Many Vikings wore a hammer amulet as a talisman to ward off bad luck, and they often greeted each other with the sign of the hammer—a raised fist, meant to convey a blessing. Viking brides wore red to their weddings as a tribute to Thor's favorite color.

Thor played a large part in Norse mythology. In one story, he fought the giant, Hrungir, who was armed with a stone shield and a flint missile. Thor flung his hammer and the giant his flint. The two met in mid-air; the hammer went on to shatter Hrungir's head, but one piece of the stone lodged in Thor's forehead. Thor could then always kindle lightning off the imbedded flint.

The worship of Thor proved to be Christianity's biggest obstacle as it spread throughout Scandinavia.

Little Redheaded Riding Hood

All right, the title is changed around a bit, but it is merely to prove a point—this simple, children's fairy tale is, in reality, a poetic retelling of a solar myth.

After Christianity established a firm foothold and its practice became standardized, there was no longer a need to graft its beliefs onto the existing religious framework. Yet for a rural populace that was still largely illiterate, a need existed to explain the mysteries of nature in symbolic terms. It would have been heresy to openly preach sun worship. Storytellers took the ancient legends and covered them with a protective layer of allegory. As time passed, scientific reasoning became more sure of itself in explaining how the cosmos operated. The fairy tales then became separated from their original purpose and were eventually passed off as harmless children's stories. *Little Red Riding Hood* affords us an example of how this transformation occurred. The story in its present form surfaced in the 16th century, and several early, illustrated versions picture the heroine with red hair under her cap.

As the story begins, "Once upon a time there lived a little girl who was loved by everyone, especially her grandmother, who made her a little hood of red velvet and called her by that name. One day her mother gave Little Red Riding Hood some cakes and honey to take to her grandmother who had become ill." The little tyke set out to visit the old woman who lived in a house in the far-off woods. While on the way, she met a wolf, and when asked where she was going, Little Red naively gave him an honest answer.

The wolf wanted to eat Red Riding Hood immediately, but then realized he could also snack on her grandmother as well. He persuaded Little Red Riding Hood to tarry a while to smell the proverbial roses while he raced off to grandmother's house, where he knocked on the door. When let inside, the wolf sprang upon the lady and swallowed her in one gulp. He put on the old woman's clothes, and streched himself out in her bed to wait for Little Red. When she came to the door, she was frightened to hear such a hoarse voice greeting her. But she thought her grandmother simply had a cold and went inside to put the cakes and honey on a shelf. What then followed is that classic refrain we all know and love:

"Grandmother, what great arms you have."
"The better to hug you, my child."
"Grandmother, what great ears you have."
"The better to hear you, my child."
"Grandmother, what great eyes you have."
"The better to see you, my child."
"Grandmother, what great teeth you have!"
"The better to eat you!!"

With these words the wolf fell upon Little Red Riding Hood and swallowed her in one big bite. Thinking he had done enough for a day, the wolf went back to bed to snooze off his meal. By chance, a hunter happened to pass the cottage and heard the snoring. Curious, he went to the house and found the rather bloated wolf fast asleep. He took a pair of scissors and snipped him open. Out jumped Little Red Riding Hood and her grandmother, both slightly slimy, but nonetheless in good shape. Needless to say, they all lived happily ever after.

This type of legend about an animal devouring a child of brightness is very widespread in ancient cultures. In Hindu mythology, a great dragon took the place of a wolf. Viewed as a sun myth, the story of Little Red Riding Hood is full of beauty and meaning. She is symbolic of the crimson evening sun, which is similar to the description given to Cuchullain's hair. The old grandmother is the earth to whom the sun brings comfort. The wolf is the blackness of night. First he devours the grandmother in darkness, and then he does the same for the evening sun. His loud snoring represents the storm winds of night that alert the hunter, which is the morning sun in strength and majesty. He slays the wolf, revives Grandmother Earth and brings Little Red Riding Hood to life again. As Paul Harvey would say, "That's the rest of the story."

For all of its technical wizardry, modern society has created no substitutes to equal the poetry and imagery of early cultures in explaining the mystery of the sun cycle. This is the reason the old myths are retold—they are too deeply imbedded in our psyche to forget. They will continue to be retold as long as the sun shines in the heavens and redheads walk upon the earth.

A Hymn to the Sun from the Hindu Rig-Veda

O Surya, with the golden hair, ascend for us day
after day, still bringing purer innocence.
Bless us with shine, bless us with perfect daylight
bless us with cold, with fervent heat and lustre.
Bestow on us, O Surya, varied riches to bless us
in our home, and when we travel.

4

A Rouge Gallery of Redheads

When red-haired people are above a certain social grade, their hair is auburn.

Mark Twain

Rascals and rogues, poets and priests, redheads have made their mark on history in many different ways. There are those such as Christopher Columbus who by dint of courage and foresight forever changed the course of human events, and those redheads such as Lizzie Borden who violently succumbed to the emotions of anger and hatred. No matter what their contribution, a certain fascination arose within me concerning well-known redheads. It was a way to bolster my own sense of "red pride" while also discovering some of the personality traits that make redheads tick. The redheads that are included in the next two chapters are by no means a complete list. Their lives, however, help to illustrate some of the high and low points that are part of the redheaded experience. Those who were successful triumphed over despair and approached life with energy and enthusiasm. In one respect they could be considered heroes, for as their lives illustrate, being a hero consists of trying the utmost to be oneself.

It is fun to think what effect these redheads had on each other. Some crossed paths at key moments in their lives. Others were involved in the same career, or were admirers of each others talent. Did they feel a certain redheaded kinship? Perhaps. History doesn't say for certain, but the next time you meet a redhead, just think what effect he or she has on you!

Jesus Christ

He is without doubt the greatest redhead of history. Nowhere, however, in the Christian Bible is there mention of Christ's hair color. Indeed, hardly any mention at all is made of his life before He began His ministry at age 30. So, for a claim to be made that Jesus Christ had red hair, an extraordinary source must be found. Such a source is Edgar Cayce, "the Sleeping Prophet."

Cayce's life is remarkable in itself. The son of a Kentucky farmer, he lived from 1877 to 1945 and achieved wide fame diagnosing illnesses and prescribing effective treatment while in a trance-state. His trances also dealt with reincarnation, Atlantis and religious beliefs.

Relying on his psychic powers, Cayce answered a number of questions pertaining to the life of Jesus Christ. He described Him as having blue eyes, a weight of 170 pounds, and hair that was "a golden brown, a yellow red." Cayce elaborated on Christ's missing years in great detail, saying that much of his information was actually recorded but then lost in the fire that destroyed the Library of Alexandria in Egypt.

According to the readings, both Mary and Joseph were members of a sect known as the Essenes, a Jewish religious order that practiced benevolence and charity. Essene philosophy incorporated many Greek and Hindu teachings concerning man's role on earth. When Mary gave birth to Jesus, she was 16 and Joseph was 36. Following their flight into Egypt, they stayed there for several years and then returned to Palestine, where Jesus was schooled in Essene thought and practice. During the missing years, Cayce said Christ also traveled to study in Egypt, Persia and India. Other details which Cayce supplied about this period were that Christ had two brothers and a sister, and that Joseph died while Christ was traveling in Persia.

When asked about events actually stated in the Gospels, Cayce elaborated on them in further detail. For instance, Christ's robe at the Last Supper was pearl gray. It was a gift from Martha, the wife of Nicodemus.

Were Cayce's readings idle dreams or true visions? Each person must answer that question for himself. But before dismissing as outlandish the thought that Jesus Christ was a redhead, consider the fact that Christ was descended from the line of David, and Biblical references to the renowned Jewish king portray him as having red hair and a ruddy complexion. Then consider a contemporary of Jesus whom legend also describes as a redhead—Judas Iscariot.

Cleopatra

The great Roman leader, Julius Caesar, was sitting in the palace of Alexandria when a slave entered his room carrying a carpet over his shoulder. "Here is a gift from my master," said the slave as he unrolled the carpet. Caesar was dumbfounded, for out of the carpet rolled the most beautiful woman he had ever seen—Cleopatra, Queen of Egypt.

So often pictured as a vile seductress, she was in reality an astute politician who tried to keep her nation sovereign by influencing the wills of two of the most powerful men in history, Julius Caesar and Mark Antony.

Cleopatra was a Macedonian, descended from the general, Ptolomy, who three hundred years earlier fought with Alexander the Great, and received Egypt as his province when Alexander died. Her likeness appeared on several coins, but the best description comes from her personal doctor, "She was lithe, not very tall and her hair was a reddish amber." Cleopatra had intelligence as well as beauty. The Greek writer, Plutarch, observed, "Her form, coupled with the persuasiveness of her conversation and her delightful style of behavior—all these produced a blend of magic."

Her unceremonious dumping at the feet of Caesar occurred in 48 B.C. when she was 21. Caesar had gone to Egypt with 4,000 troops to ostensibly settle a civil war between Cleopatra and her brother. But his real purpose was to add Egypt to the expanding Roman Empire. Since her brother's troops held Alexandria and had orders to slay her on sight, the carpet subterfuge was the only way she could gain Caesar's presence.

From all accounts, Caesar was delighted by the ruse. The two became lovers and after her brother's defeat, Caesar showed his love by naming Cleopatra a queen instead of annexing Egypt as a Roman province. Cleopatra in turn, bore Caesar a son named Caesarion, and when Caesar returned in triumph to Rome, she followed with a retinue of slaves, soldiers and opulence that created a sensation when she entered the city.

Everything Cleopatra hoped for was coming true. Her throne in Egypt was secure and she was the mother of Caesar's only natural son. It seemed inevitable that Caesar would divorce his wife, Calpurnia, and marry Cleopatra, thus uniting the power of Rome with the culture and riches of Egypt.

Neither she nor Caesar had reckoned with the bitterness some Romans felt upon seeing their Republic wither away. A conspiracy of senators was formed, and Caesar was stabbed to death on the fateful Ides of March in 44 B.C. Upon hearing the news, Cleopatra sensed the danger she would be in and returned to Egypt. Since Caesar's death was so unexpected, he left no will legitimizing Caesarion. Instead, when the will was read by Marc Antony in the Senate, three-quarters of his estate went to a little-known great-nephew, Octavion. Although Marc Antony was the more powerful general, Octavion, later known as Augustus, was

Caesar's heir and thus commanded great loyalty. The two formed an uneasy truce and proceeded to quash the armies of Caesar's enemies.

From the safety of Egypt, Cleopatra watched this civil war rage. She knew one man would eventually emerge victorious, and in her mind, that man was Marc Antony. Antony had won a great victory over Caesar's enemies at Phillippi, in Greece, and his star was ascending. Octavion, meanwhile, was viewed as a pale and sickly youth.

A bold leader in battle, Marc Antony was a dissolute wastrel in private. So, when he summoned Cleopatra, she went willingly, knowing full-well that although Marc Antony conquered armies, she conquered men. Cleopatra was 28 at the time, and at the height of her beauty and charm. Marc Antony was in Asia Minor, and she sailed to meet him in a gilded barge with purple sails, and oars capped by inlaid silver. To Mark Antony, the soldier, it was a vision of heaven.

Cleopatra's victory over him was complete. The two left for Alexandria and Marc Antony soon wasted away in undreamed of luxury. For instance, at one of her parties, Cleopatra took a valuable pearl earring, dissolved it in vinegar, and then had it served as a drink.

Cleopatra had every hope that Alexandria would surpass Rome and become the seat of the Empire, with herself as Queen. She bore Marc Antony three children, and watched in triumph as Antony celebrated his victory over the Armenians in Alexandria, not Rome. This action was too much for the Romans to accept. It blatantly defied Roman tradition, and threatened to eclipse the City's importance. The Romans felt neurotically insecure, and Octavion capitalized on this fear through a skillful propaganda campaign against Cleopatra. The Roman poet, Horace, set the tone by characterizing her as a "Fatal Monster."

Antony was not nearly as skillful a politician as Julius Caesar. Caesar never forgot that the first rule of government is to govern, while Antony believed in using the riches of a country for his pleasure. Octavion was thus able to consolidate political and military power to challenge Antony for sole control of the Empire. When the two clashed at the naval Battle of Actium in 31 B.C., Antony's forces were defeated. The great soldier abandoned the battle early to follow Cleopatra's barge back to Egypt. Whether it was cowardice or a realization that the battle was lost which caused him to flee will never be known. But, in either case, the end was near. When his soldiers deserted as Octavion closed in upon Alexandria, Marc Antony committed suicide.

Cleopatra also tried to kill herself, but Octavion's soldiers prevented it. She was taken to Octavion and the two viewed each other for the first time. Cleopatra sadly realized that here was one man she could not control. Nearly 40, her dreams of empire lay dead upon the graves of two men. But she still had her queenly pride, and she was not going to be dragged to Rome in chains as a bauble of Octavion's victory. At the tomb of Marc Antony she cried, "Hide me with thee under the earth of Egypt."

The night before she was to leave for Rome, a farmer came to the palace with a basket of figs. He delivered them to Cleopatra, who reached inside the basket and was bitten by a poisonous asp hidden in the bottom. When the guards realized what had happened, it was too late. Clad in royal robes, she died upon a golden couch. Her servant, Charmion, murmured, "It is well done and worthy of a queen, the descendant of so many kings."

Eric the Red and Leif the Lucky

If a Real Estate Hustlers Hall of Fame is ever created, Eric the Red will surely be its charter member, for all of the outlandish schemes that have been created by purveyors of swampland pale into insignificance compared to the panache of this Viking in naming a 96,000-square-mile sheet of ice "Greenland." This touch of showmanship befitted the personality of a man who is remembered as one of history's great explorers; a leader of courage, daring, and unfortunately, a fiery temper.

This latter trait, in fact, is what got him started on his voyage. After a quarrel with a neighbor in Iceland, Eric instructed his hired men to loosen a landslide on the man's house. A feud naturally started, and Eric killed two of the victim's kinsmen. As punishment, the Viking assembly banished him to another portion of Iceland. Within months, Eric killed three other men following an argument over household possessions. This savage behavior was too much for even the rough-and-tumble Vikings to handle. The assembly exiled him for three years, starting in 981 A.D. During this time, he would be put to death if he were to return to Iceland.

With this ruling as an incentive, Eric loaded a ship with 20 trusted friends and relatives to sail in hopes of finding a rumored group of rocky islands west of Iceland. Eric did not find the islands, but he did encounter a stretch of ice-covered shoreline and giant glaciers. He turned his ship south and after rounding the tip of the ice mass he encountered a temperate, grassy area that could supply pasture for animals. The next three years were spent charting and mapping this new land. When his exile ended, Eric returned to Iceland with his "sales pitch" ready. The *Flateyjarbok,* a contemporary historical account, noted, "He called the land Greenland, for, he said that many men would desire to visit if he gave the land a good name."

Eric certainly knew his market. Iceland was becoming overcrowded. Combined with the adventuresome Viking spirit, Eric was soon able to persuade over a thousand pioneers to join him in colonizing Greenland. In the summer of 986 A.D., 25 ships set sail with provisions, tools and livestock to begin a new life. Only 14 survived the voyage, while the others were capsized by huge waves generated by an underwater volcano. Upon arriving, Eric assigned each ship to a fjord, and the settlers began carving out a new life. Eric had earlier chosen the choicest parcel of land

for himself. It extended for nearly a half-mile along a fjord and was a quarter-mile wide. He built his house of sod, and he also constructed a barn that could house 30 cows.

Now that he was a man of property, Eric's hotheadedness had dissipated and he proved to be an excellent ruler. The colony prospered under his leadership, and the settlers traded furs and ivory to Norway for much-needed grain and iron. Eric's son Leif, another redhead, had come of age during the development of the Greenland colony. He had inherited his father's leadership abilities but little of his temper, and Eric began entrusting him to lead the trading voyages.

On one of these trips, Leif was converted to Christianity and brought back a priest with him to Christianize Greenland. The whole settlement, except Eric, accepted the new religion. Stubbornly, he clung to his old pagan beliefs and, as a result, his wife refused to sleep with him. About the time Eric's marital troubles were occurring, Leif heard from other Vikings that more land existed to the west of Greenland. At the age of 23, Leif used his trading profits to buy his own boat to search for these new lands. Eric was to accompany him (perhaps to get away from his wife), but on the way to the harbor he injured his foot when his horse slipped and threw him to the ground. Interpreting this as an omen, Eric refused to go. He was quoted as saying to Leif, "It is not my fate to find more lands than this where we now dwell. You and I may no longer follow together."

As sole leader, Leif, and 35 followers, set sail westward around the year 1,000 A.D. Within days they sighted what described as "a land which was like one great slab of rock. It seemed to be a worthless country." Judging from the current patterns in that part of the Atlantic, the adventurers may have seen the coast of Labrador. Although they put ashore, Leif and his party did not stay long. They sailed to another land, most likely Nova Scotia, which Leif described as being "level land, completely wooded." He named the area "Markland" (Forest Land) and once again set off.

The exact location of his third landfall has had scholars arguing for decades. Various locations such as Cape Cod, Rhode Island and New Jersey have been suggested for the site of Leif's legendary "Vinland." Wherever it was, Leif and his crew harbored for the winter and explored the countryside. Grapes were discovered in abundance, and the crews filled their cargo hold with the fruit, along with timber, which was in great demand at home. On the way back to Greenland, Leif rescued a crew of shipwrecked Vikings and added their cargo to his own. Leif thus returned a wealthy man. Because of his good fortune, he acquired the name, "Leif the Lucky."

His Vinland adventure was to be his last, for Eric the Red died soon after his return, and Leif assumed the hereditary role of chieftain until his death in 1020 A.D.

Queen Isabella

The course of history is often changed by fateful years and coincidences. Rarely, however, has the fate of the Western World been changed so radically in the same year by two redheads. Yet that is what happened in 1492, a year in which Spain defeated the Moors, expelled the Jews, and dispatched Christopher Columbus on his search for a trade route to China by sailing west across the Atlantic. Dispensing her blessing on the voyage was Columbus' fellow redhead and patron, Queen Isabella of Spain.

In many respects, her reign was a precursor to the reign of another redhead, Queen Elizabeth I of England. For as Elizabeth later did for England, Isabella politically united her country, removed a threat of foreign domination, presided over a "Golden Age" of the arts and supported a bloody religious persecution.

The Spain which Isabella would one day rule was a divided country at the time of her birth in 1451. Although the Moslems had been forced out from much of the Iberian

Peninsula, they still held the rich, southern province of Granada. The Kingdom of Aragon embraced the eastern part of the peninsula while Isabella's land of Castille occupied the central part and northern coast.

Isabella fought a civil war in 1475 against her older sister, Juana, to gain the throne. She was helped in this venture by the political and military power of her husband, Prince Ferdinand of Aragon, whom she had secretly married six years earlier. When Juana's forces were defeated in 1479, she retired to a convent and allowed Isabella, then 28, to ascend to the throne unchallenged.

Although no great beauty, the new queen had pleasingly-plump features, with blue-green eyes and long, copper-red hair. She truly loved Ferdinand even though their marriage was politically motivated. For the most part, Isabella was a contemplative person who spent much of her time praying or reading.

She was also a farsighted and firm ruler who put her duties to country before personal pleasure. Isabella gave special tax breaks to Spanish printers to produce books and thus spread the growth of learning. The sons of merchants and tradesmen were allowed entry to universities for the first time. Classical masterpieces were translated by scholars into Spanish, thus fostering the Spanish Renaissance. Isabella was determined that her country should participate in the new wave of art and literature sweeping Europe.

The growth of culture, however, did not occur until there was peace in the land. Following the civil war, Isabella organized a nationwide vigilante force, called the Santa Hernandad, which caught, tried and executed bandits who had flourished during the breakdown of civil law. She also razed many feudal castles and formed a standing army of men to prevent the nobility from attempting a revolt on Juana's behalf. But Isabella was not a political despot. While judging crimes committed in Seville during the civil war, she ordered a general pardon for all offenses save the grave crime of heresy.

It was in the area of religion that Isabella was unyielding. She sought to establish a religiously-pure Spain, and thought it her divinely-inspired duty to advance Catholicism. Anti-Semitism was not only tolerated, it was encouraged. Jews converted to Catholicism to avoid persecution, but many secretly maintained their religious rituals. They were called "conversos," and some had reached positions of great wealth and prominence. Thus, greed and envy, combined with Isabella's narrow view of purity, brought on the Spanish Inquisition. Beginning in 1483, with the appointment of Isabella's former personal priest, Tomas de Torquemada, as Inquisitor-General, the Inquisition proceeded in a barbarous fashion that saw thousands of conversos burned at the stake, or tortured, and their property confiscated. Those Jews who did not convert obviously could not be charged with heresy. Instead, their property also was confiscated, and about one hundred and fifty thousand were expelled from Spain in 1492.

Ironically, the stolen Jewish wealth provided the financing for Ferdinand and Isabella's two greatest triumphs—the conquest of the Moors and the voyage of Christopher Columbus.

The fight against the Moors began in 1481, and it occupied much of Ferdinand and Isabella's time and treasury. Again, religion was a motivating factor. Isabella wrote a letter to the Pope in which she explained, "Thus we can hope that the holy Catholic faith may be spread and Christendom of so unremitting a menace as abides here at our gates." Isabella served as Ferdinand's supply officer, often spending time with the armies in the field. More than anything else, the Moorish war created a unified Spain. Castilians and Aragonese fought beside each other and, when final victory occurred in January, 1492, Granada returned to Christian rule for the first time in seven hundred and eighty-one years. When the two monarchs entered the City of Alhambre in triumph, the crowds shouted out, "Granada for Ferdinand and Isabella." One of those watching the procession was Christopher Columbus.

Isabella first met Columbus in 1486 when he was 34 and she was 35. Although she fancied the idea of sailing west to China on the chance of spreading Christianity and opening trade routes, she did not think the project very feasible. Ferdinand totally opposed the idea. Besides, there was no money to spare on such an expedition. Rather than abandon the idea entirely, however, Isabella gave Columbus a small annual stipend. Following the annexation of Granada, she and Ferdinand were again willing to listen to Columbus. Isabella agreed to spend the equivalant of a few thousand dollars on the expedition, feeling she had nothing to lose. So on August 3, 1492, the newly appointed Admiral of the Ocean Seas set out on his history-making voyage. Upon his return, the two most powerful rulers in Europe rose to greet him, an almost unprecedented tribute.

Isabella would live to see Columbus make several more voyages. The results of his discoveries poured a flood of unimaginable wealth into Spain. She would also see her dream of a religiously-united domain come true when she felt the country was politically powerful enough to expel the Moors in 1502. It was one of her last important decrees. Queen Isabella I died on November 26, 1504, at the age of 53. History has linked her name with cruelty and grandeur. In her own heart, Isabella was totally sincere in believing her actions were carrying out God's will.

Upon hearing of her death, Columbus wrote to his son, Diego, "Her life was always holy and ready for all things of His holy service, and for this reason it may be believed she is in His holy glory and beyond the desires of this rough and wearisome world."

Christopher Columbus

Outside of Union Station in Washington, D.C., stands a marble memorial to Christopher Columbus which has as its inscription:

To the Memory of
Christopher Columbus
Whose High Faith
and
Indomitable Courage
Gave to Mankind
A New World

No finer tribute can be voiced, for although it is now doubtful that Columbus was the first European to encounter the New World, his greatest contribution to humanity lies not so much in what he discovered, but in what he provided—hope. Into a Europe that was suffering from political , economic and spiritual stagnation, he sparked a tinder that flamed into a Renaissance of thought and institutions that is still glowing to this very day. It was a gift that transformed the course of human events, and a gift that was born of bravery, perseverance and faith in God.

The possessor of these qualities was a Genoese sailor born in 1451. There are only scanty records of Columbus' early life. His father was a master weaver, and it seems probable that Columbus started his sailing career by shipping his father's products in coastal vessels along the Italian peninsula. Records do show that he was a member of a Genoese naval fleet that fought against the Portugese in 1475. Columbus' vessel was sunk during the battle, and he only managed to save himself by holding onto a piece of wooden debris and swimming six miles to the Portugese shore. Penniless and ill-at-ease in this unfriendly country, Columbus shipped out again almost immediately on a merchant ship bound for Iceland. Much speculation has arisen from this little-known voyage, for it is thought Columbus may have encountered stories about Leif Ericson's earlier trips to Vinland. By the time he returned in 1477, Portugal was again at peace and Columbus settled in the bustling seaport of Lisbon. He went into the mapmaking business, a lucrative trade due to Portugal's extensive explorations along the African Coast, and married the daughter of a prominent local family. By her he had a son, Diego, who would become his trusted confidante and successor. Following her death around 1485, Columbus had an affair three years later with a Spanish woman who bore his second son, Ferdinand, who wrote his father's biography.

While he was in Portugal, Columbus conceived what he termed "The Enterprise of the Indies," which, as every school child knows, consisted of sailing west to reach the riches of the East. In addition to opening new trade routes, he hoped to spread Christianity, as well as make a tidy profit for himself in the process. Contrary to the popular myth, Columbus did not have to prove the world was round. A spherical earth was an idea well-accepted in the leading universities of Europe. Columbus had trouble with the distances involved. He favored a large land mass and a narrow ocean, and believed it was a distance of 2,400 miles from Europe to Japan while, in reality, it is nearly 11,000 miles. Because of this uneasiness about mileage, the Portugese government turned down his request to sponsor a voyage of discovery.

Undaunted, he and Diego boarded a ship to bring their idea to Spain. A series of fortuitous friendships allowed him to arrange an audience with King Ferdinand and fellow redhead Queen Isabella in May of 1486. Columbus at that time was 35 and described as "tall, blue-eyed and redheaded, and a gentleman of great force of spirit, of lofty thoughts and endowed with forbearance in the hardships and adversities that were always occurring." His dignity, sincerity and absolute self-confidence favorably impressed Queen Isabella, although she was occupied by the more pressing war against the Moors. With uncanny foresight she retained Columbus' interest by paying him a retainer of about 90 dollars a year. This amount, the salary of an average seaman, helped him to survive, but the inaction of the next six years formed a dark period in his life that he rarely chose to discuss.

Finally, just as he was about to abandon hope on Spain and travel to France with his plans, the Moorish war ended and Isabella supported his expedition at the cost of roughly twenty thousand dollars.

Armed with credentials naming him Admiral of the Ocean Sea, and contracts to outfit his ships, Columbus left the queen and went to the port city of Palos. Sadly, another myth at this point must be dispelled. Isabella did not "hock" her crown jewels to support Columbus. The boats he chartered were owed to the crown because of back taxes. On August 3, 1492, the *Nina, Pinta* and *Santa Maria,* with a total complement of 90 men, set sail on one of the greatest voyages in maritime history.

Columbus first stopped at the Canary Islands before proceeding westward. His crew consisted mostly of able-bodied sailors with a few prisoners to fill out the list. After several weeks at sea, they grew mutinous, not because of fear of falling off the edge of the world, but because the constant westward wind made them wonder how they would ever return. On October 10, the men were so rebellious that Columbus promised to return if they did not sight land in two days. As fate would have it, the island of San Salvador was reached on October 12. To the total wonderment of the local Taino tribe, Columbus landed on shore with a contingent of men and claimed the island in the name of Ferdinand and Isabella. Columbus was much impressed by the generosity of the natives and they in turn were delighted by the red caps and glass beads he distributed as trade goods.

After the initial landfall, Columbus further explored the Caribbean, sighting such islands as Cuba, where he tried to find the Great Khan, and Hispaniola, where he lost the *Santa Maria* on a shoal on Christmas Eve. This latter setback forced him to establish a colony, since the two remaining ships did not have enough room for everyone to return to Europe. Many of the 40 men left behind were actually eager to stay, for gold was found on the island and they wanted to be the first to exploit it. Columbus returned to Europe bringing gold, Indians, parrots and syphilis. This latter "gift" was in many ways repayment for the diseases and slavery that Europe exported to the New World.

His arrival in Spain in 1493 created a sensation. The King and Queen were fascinated by his adventures, and immediately agreed to his plans for a second voyage. A fleet of 17 vessels and nearly 1,200 volunteers sailed in October, 1493, to colonize the new realms. The easy passage they enjoyed deceptively masked the hardships that were to follow. The colony he had left behind was wiped out by the natives because of the Spaniards' lust for women and gold. Despite this setback, Columbus began a second colony, which he named Isabella, for the Queen. In many respects, this second voyage proved to be the high point of his career. After he changed the roles of Sea Lord for that of Viceroy, things rapidly deteriorated for him. His colonists wanted to search for gold instead of tending to crops and building a city. They soon became dissatisfied with the hard life and, when Columbus left for further explorations, a representative from the Crown arrived and was deluged by complaints and accusations. Columbus had to accept partial responsibility for the unrest, for it was his suggestion to start up a slave trade and enforce gold tribute from the Indians. He also failed to punish the Spaniards responsible for gross crimes against the natives, who had until then been peaceful.

In order to counter what was sure to be a damaging report, Columbus returned to Spain in the spring of 1496. Upon landing at Cadiz he adopted the coarse brown habit of a monk in the belief that his misfortune was a chastisement from God. Fortunately, he still had the respect of the King and Queen, and they agreed to a third voyage. However, the early enthusiasm was now lacking, and it took two years for this new fleet to sail. Three of the ships were to replenish the colony and the other three were to be used for exploration. In command of these latter vessels, Columbus discovered the coast of South America, touching shore near the mouth of the Ornico River. The presence of Indians bearing pearls convinced Columbus this was truly China, since Marco Polo had earlier written about the pearls the Great Khan possessed.

Had he returned to Spain at this point his voyage would have been a triumph, but instead he landed in the new city of Santo Domingo to find the political situation a disaster. His brother, Bartholomew, had failed to quell an outright rebellion. When Columbus arrived he was forced to hang seven of the mutineers. As luck would have it, a commissioner from Spain arrived the same day and upon entering the harbor and seeing the bodies swaying from the gibbet, he immediately held Columbus at fault and sent him home in chains.

Dispirited and impoverished, Columbus presented himself to the monarchs who had so faithfully supported him in the past. A court historian wrote, "The Admiral went to kiss the hands of the King and Queen, and with tears made his apologies as well as he could. When they heard him, with much clemency they consoled him and spoke such words that he was somewhat content." In truth, Isabella realized Columbus was hopeless as an administrator, but she still valued his skill as a mariner, so she consented to support a fourth voyage of exploration.

This trip, which was to be Columbus' last, began with four ships in May of 1502. After weathering a hurricane, he proceeded to the coastline of Central America where he traded for gold. Bad wind and weather plagued him for nearly a month. What was worse, his ships' hulls were rotting away from sea worms. One ship had to be abandoned, and the other two barely reached uncolonized Jamaica. Since nobody knew where they were, their only hope of rescue lay in the plan of reaching Santo Domingo by a 100-

mile canoe trip. The canoes arrived, but due to political infighting, it took eight months to rescue the sailors. When he finally returned to Spain, crippled by arthritis and failing health, he knew that he would never cross the seas again. His last days were spent in a feeble attempt to claim what he felt were his just revenues from what he still firmly believed was China. Finally on May 20, 1506, Columbus took his final voyage, sailing away on the ebb tide.

Queen Elizabeth I

Standing before the troops gathered to fight the Spanish Armada, Queen Elizabeth spoke out, "I know that I have the body of a weak and feeble woman; but I have the heart of a King, and a King of England, too!"

Ruthless as a pirate, coy as a courtesan, Elizabeth I was one of the greatest queens and redheads England has ever known.

The period of her rule was called a "Golden Age," but it could as well have been known as a "Crimson Age" for all the blood that was shed, starting with her own mother. Elizabeth was born September 7, 1533, the illegitimate daughter of Henry VIII and Ann Boleyn. The incredibly complex politics of the time centered around producing a male heir to carry on the line and thus avoid civil war. Henry had Anne Boleyn beheaded, ostensibly for adultery, but really to enable him to wed Jane Seymour, by whom he fathered a son, Edward VII. But Henry, Edward and Elizabeth's older sister, Mary, were all to die of natural causes, paving the way for Elizabeth's coronation on January 15, 1559.

She was well-prepared for ruling. A contemporary described her by saying, "The constitution of her mind is exempt from female weakness, and she is endowed with a masculine power of application. No apprehension can be quicker than hers, no memory more retentive. French and Italian she speaks like English."

Her coronation was an elaborate affair that appealed to her sense of pomp. On her red hair sat a golden crown, and she was carried by her servants in a gold-embroidered litter from which she was able to speak to the crowds. Elizabeth was shrewd enough to court the people's support, because she knew the cunning and treachery that existed among the royalty, including those who were her advisors.

From the beginning of her reign until her last years, Elizabeth had to contend with these avaricious men, along with the problems of religion, marriage, conspiracy and Mary, Queen of Scots.

The first issue to surface was that of religion. Henry VIII had broken with Rome over the question of divorce and established the Anglican Church. His daughter, Mary, however, was a Catholic. The populace wanted to know in which direction Elizabeth would turn. She swore to uphold the rights of the Catholic Church during her coronation, but quickly disregarded her oath to ally herself with Protestantism.

Powerful nobles, who had helped her father confiscate Catholic monastaries, and a populace dissatisfied with the Pope, backed her decision. On June 24, 1559, an absolute prohibition on saying the Mass was issued. At first, this was hardly enforced. But later in her reign, as political intrigues and rebellions centering aroung Catholicism surfaced, Elizabeth ordered a brutal suppression of the religion, especially centering on the Jesuit missionaries who had entered England to revive the faith. In all, 150 priests and lay people were put to death, and 500 more died in prison.

Much of the Catholic unrest centered around Mary, Queen of Scots. Mary was the granddaughter of Henry's sister, Margaret, and had a powerful claim upon the throne due to Elizabeth's illegitimacy. The death of Mary's husband, the King of France, forced her to return to Scotland in August, 1561. The Catholic Queen soon encountered the fierce hostility of Protestants such as John Knox. After being accused of complicity in the murder of her second husband, Mary fled for her life to England on May 16, 1568.

Arriving dishevelled, she asked Elizabeth for some clothes and received a torn dress, two pieces of black velvet and a pair of shoes. Mary was ordered to the Tower of London and she remained in custody for 19 years. Elizabeth was clearly perplexed by what to do with Mary. In 1572 she asked her advisors, "Can I put to death the bird, who, to escape the pursuit of the hawk, has fled to my feet for protection?"

On the one hand, Elizabeth was loath to kill a fellow monarch. But on the other, Mary posed a clear threat to her throne by being a focal point of Catholic unrest. Indeed, in 1569, Elizabeth's forces had to suppress a rebellion of the northern English counties where supporters intended to put Mary on the throne and restore Catholicism. The issue came to a head in 1586 when Elizabeth's advisors accused Mary of fomenting a plot to kidnap Elizabeth and gain the throne herself. Asked whether the death sentence should be carried out, Elizabeth shouted, "By God I do!" So, on February 7, 1587, the Scottish Queen was beheaded. To appease the populace who were recoiling at the thought of a queen being executed, she spent forty thousand pounds sterling on her funeral.

Mary's death, coupled with an English army fighting in the Netherlands, as well as incessant harassment of Spanish treasure convoys by English pirates, provided Phillip of Spain with the justification to invade England and restore the Catholic faith. Thirty years earler he had proposed marriage to Elizabeth, and therein lies one of the enigmas of her reign. Why she never married has led to several theories. One contended that she could never make up her mind. Another suggests that Elizabeth shrewdly realized that the only way she could keep her independence was by leading-on her powerful suitors by not saying "yes," but never quite saying "no," and thus keeping all of them at odds with each other.

A third theory was that Elizabeth was actually a man. This would explain the losing of much of her hair at age 30 and her coarse manners and temper. But it does not explain why Henry VIII did not embrace Elizabeth as his much-needed son. The answer to this question will probably never be known, but the results of Phillip's invasion plans are recorded forever in English history.

The Spanish Armada was defeated in the summer of 1588 by a combination of bad weather and the crafty English seamanship by Sir Francis Drake, who loosed flaming fireships on the Spanish while they were anchored for the night. Some historians felt the victory would have been even more complete had Elizabeth not been so scrimping in supplying the fleet with ammunition.

This frugality was characteristic of her reign. One of the reasons the populace respected her was that she did not raise taxes. But then again, despite all the praise paid to her by the writers of the period, she was loathe to spend a farthing to support the arts. Her interests ran more towards cock-fighting and bull-baiting.

It would be nice to think that following the defeat of the Spanish Armada, the remainder of Elizabeth's reign would be one of untroubled tranquility and prosperity. But unfortunately, such was not the case. The most wrenching revolt of her monarchy occurred in 1601. The Earl of Essex was a personal favorite of the Queen, and many felt she loved him. She dispatched Essex to Ireland to put down a revolt. Having little success, and feeling the Queen's advisors were plotting against him, he returned to England and attempted to raise the citizens of London to march with him and oust her advisors. Such treason cost Essex his head in 1601.

Elizabeth's own death occurred two years later on March 24, 1603. Her once-strong health failed her and her spirits became depressed. The problem of succession remained with her to the last. While on her deathbed, she gave feeble consent to James, son of Mary, Queen of Scots, to ascend to the throne as King of England. The succession had come full circle.

George Washington

The situation looked desperate. French soldiers were pouring a murderous crossfire into tiny, hastily-built Fort Necessity near the present city of Uniontown, Pennsylvania. The young Virginia colonel saw that a third of his demoralized men were either dead or wounded, and the rest were fighting in a drenching rain, with dwindling ammunition. George Washington was trapped and surrender was the only way out. At midnight he raised a white flag and negotiated a truce whereby his 200 remaining soldiers were allowed to return home unharmed. The date, which meant nothing to him at the time, was July 4.

This defeat in 1754 was a bitter one for Washington, for he had no way of knowing that the experience he gained as a frontier soldier in the French and Indian War would enable him one day to command a ragtag force of volunteers against a powerful British army during the American Revolutionary War.

Known to history as a soldier and a statesman, Washington's later accomplishments had their roots in his early life in Virginia. He was born February 22, 1732, into a well-to-do family. Even from an early age, he was noted for his great strength. Although Mark Twain was correct when he remarked that Washington would be declared a fraud if he did not resemble his Gilbert Stuart portrait, as a youth Washington was tall, auburn-haired and powerfully built. Thomas Jefferson later described him as "the most graceful figure that could be seen on horseback." An atrocious speller in school, he nonetheless had a flair for mathematics. He soon used his talent in the profession of surveying.

His elder half-brother, Lawrence, whom he much admired, helped to get him appointed as the official surveyor of Culpepper County when he was 17 years old. Washington divided his time between laying out farms and partaking of the dances and fox hunts at Lawrence's farm, Mt. Vernon. His social contacts among the Virginia elite enabled him to be appointed in October, 1753, to carry a letter to the French military commander near Lake Erie informing him of English disapproval of French plans to expand into the Ohio River Valley. While he was meeting with the French, the Seneca Indian Chief, Half King, became so impressed with Washington that he adopted him into his tribe. It was the one bright point on the arduous trip, for the French rebuffed his message and Washington almost drowned in the ice-choked Allegheny River near present-day Pittsburgh. Washington's account of his mission circulated in the courts of Europe and caused quite a concern. To combat the growing French influence, Governor Dinwiddie of Virginia dispatched Washington in 1754 to reinforce an earlier group sent to build a fort along the Monongahela River.

While en route, Washington's men ambushed a French force and were in turn defeated at Ft. Necessity. Failing to correctly translate the French-written surrender document, Washington mistakenly said he "assassinated" the French commander. This propaganda-ploy was used to touch off the French and Indian War in America. Washington, however, did not have much time to sulk about his defeat. The next year a British army commanded by General Edward Braddock arrived to oust the French from Western Pennsylvania. While they were advancing through the wilderness, Frenchmen and their Indian allies hid behind trees and ambushed the red-uniformed British. Not knowing where to shoot, the British soldiers panicked and began a chaotic retreat. Although sick with dysentery, Washington bravely rallied troops to fight a rear-guard action. This display of courage enabled him to be named Commander of the Virginia Militia when he was only 23 years old.

After serving in the army several more years, Washington retired from the military to take up the life of a Virginia farmer. Lawrence had died, leaving him Mt. Vernon. George took up residence there and hopelessly fell in love with Sally Fairfax, the wife of his best friend. Fortunately, he was saved from embarassment when a prosperous young widow, Martha Dandridge Custis, entered his life. The two were married in January, 1759, and Washington settled down to home life with Martha and her two children. He tended to his farms, rising at 4 a.m. to oversee maintenance. He also busied himself with starting a commercial fishery along the Potomac River and attempting to domesticate an American wine grape. Always fond of card games and stories, Washington spent many an evening at the local Indian Queen Tavern with former officers. When he promised free corn-whiskey to everyone who voted for h im, Washington got himself elected to the Virginia House of Burgesses. Although not a great orator, he quickly gained the respect of his peers for his intelligent, well-thought-out opinions.

Washington became a substantial figure in the Virginia political arena by the time he was in his forties. He keenly listened to the eloquent speeches on freedom delivered by Patrick Henry, and he began identifying himself as an American, rather than a British subject. Events between England and America were fast coming to a head. Skirmishes had been fought at Lexington and Concord, and a body of colonials had captured Fort Ticonderoga in New York. When he attended the Second Congress in 1775, Washington was wearing the blue-and-buff uniform of the Virginia militia. John Adams, recognizing the need for a prominent Southerner in the army, nominated him as Commander-in Chief. He viewed this honor as a mixed blessing, confiding to Patrick Henry, "From the day I enter upon command of the American armies, I date my fall and the ruin of my reputation."

He was almost correct, for the next seven years were to witness an almost unmitigated chain of disasters. Had they been quicker, the British could have easily crushed his inexperienced army on several occasions. Plagued by shortages of supplies and money, Washington's inspiring presence was at times the only force that held the army together during such dark hours as the winter at Valley Forge.

Washington called upon his Indian fighting experience and utilized an extensive spy network to fight a war of quick strikes and long retreats. His personal courage was beyond question. In one battle he so far outraced his troops that he was nearly captured. Yet he was not hardened to the suffering caused by war. While watching a doomed rear-guard action at the Battle of Long Island, Washington cried, "My God, what brave fellows I must lose this day." Finally, when France entered the war in support of the Americans, Washington was able to use their seapower to bottle up the British at Yorktown in October, 1781, and thus effectively end the war. In retrospect, it can be said of Washington's military ability that he lost nearly every battle except the last one.

Following the war, Washington longed for nothing more than to quietly return to Mt. Vernon. But his farming years were again interrupted when he was chosen as President of the Constitutional Convention in 1787. The old Articles of Confederation were proving unworkable, and the convention was an attempt to find a better alternative. When the new Constitution was ratified, Washington was chosen as the nation's first President in 1788, and was again elected in 1792.

Washington's two terms were not easy ones, mainly because nobody had ever tried to run a government based on popular consent of the people. He walked a thin dividing-line between issues such as aristocratic aloofness versus dignity, and whether or not the executive office was given a broad range of implied powers or a strict list of circumscribed responsibilities. During his second term Washington had to prove the stability of the new government by sending troops against 7,000 Western Pennsylvania farmers who had refused to pay a federal tax on whiskey. He also labored to keep the United States from becoming involved in a new war between England and France. The strain of the two terms took their toll on Washington. He suffered two illnesses while in office and had to cope with slanderous attacks by political enemies.

The peace of Mt. Vernon again beckoned to him in 1796, and he returned to his farm for the quiet and tranquillity it afforded. One winter day in 1799, he returned, cold and wet, from riding across the fields. Complaining of a sore throat, he lay in bed and asked to be bled by leeches to improve his condition. The leeches, along with mustard packs and other remedies, failed to cure him, and Washington slipped into death on December 14, 1799.

Washington gave the United States what it truly needed, a leader who stood above the fray and allowed the disparate parts of the new country to forge a national spirit of unity. His spirit is part of the American scene, undiminished by over 200 years of history. He still remains, "First in war, first in peace, first in the hearts of his countrymen."

Thomas Jefferson

Thomas Jefferson was fond of telling his friends, "A mind always employed is always happy." By his own definition, this jack-of-all genius must have been the happiest man of recorded history. A mere listing of his accomplishments would require a book in itself, but even more importantly, Jefferson's high moral principles and political acumen formed one of the solid cornerstones of the American Republic.

Jefferson was born April 13, 1743, in rural Virginia, and from an early age he demonstrated a lively, curious attitude towards nature. Seeking to expand his knowledge, he enrolled at the College of William and Mary in Williamsburg, Va., when he was 17 years old. His professors soon recognized his brilliance, and Jefferson was asked to dine with some of the colony's leading political figures. From these dinner table debates, Jefferson gained an appreciation for the law, and after graduating from college in two years, he spent the next five interning with George Wythe, Virginia's leading lawyer. He studied both the practical aspects of preparing a courtroom case, and the deeper roots of legal history and government. Never a flamboyant orator like his friend, Patrick Henry, Jefferson was nonetheless quite successful because of his thorough, methodical approach to matters.

At this point his mind was also beginning to unfold in its myriad directions. His first major project involved clearing a navigation channel in the Rivanna River. This successful undertaking helped to get him elected to the Virginia House of Burgesses in 1769. Erect, tall and redheaded, Jefferson's physical appearance as a legislator was as impressive as his mind. He soon became one of the key figures in Virginia's support for the smoldering independence movement. Too ill to attend the First Continental Congress, Jefferson's views on freedom burst into flame at the Second Continental Congress in one of the most important documents ever written—The Declaration of Independence.

On June 7, 1776, Richard Henry Lee of Virginia introduced a motion calling for independence, but several key colonies were hesitant to back it. The measure was tabled until July 1, and a committee was appointed the next day to prepare a more formal declaration. Although some of the most brilliant men in the colonies, such as Benjamin Franklin and John Adams, were on the committee, the task of writing the document fell to 33-year-old Jefferson. Working alone in the upstairs apartment of a bricklayer's house, Jefferson drew upon his vast learning and penned, "When in the course of human events it becomes necessary for one people to dissolve the political bonds which have connected them with another . . ."

The complete writing took 17 days. It was presented to the Continental Congress for formal adoption after the group had voted on July 2 in favor of independence. The wise Benjamin Franklin turned to Jefferson as discussion began and said, "You will suffer less if you think of it as having been written by someone else." Particularly galling to Jefferson was the deletion of a section condemning slavery. For two days the declaration was debated until the delegates passed it unanimously on July 4, 1776. Four days later it was read to the people by Colonel John Nixon of Philadelphia. The bridge had been crossed. There was no turning back.

Jefferson's involvement with the Congress past this point became minimal. He returned to Virginia and busily set about his duties as a legislator in the House of Burgesses. He championed land reform bills, bills advocating religious freedom, and a revision of the criminal laws that would sanction the death penalty only for crimes of murder and treason. Jefferson abhorred capital punishment, calling it "the last melancholy resource against those whose existence has become inconsistent with the safety of their fellow citizens." He took little part in the war effort, not due to a lack of courage, but because of little personal interest in military glory. Jefferson instead served as governor in 1780 and 1781. These two years were the worst of his political career. He was severely criticized for his feeble response to British invasionary forces which attacked Richmond and very nearly captured the entire legislature.

Jefferson was only too happy to retire to his home, Monticello, near Charlottesville, and care for Martha, his beloved wife of 10 years, who was quite ill. Following her death in September, 1782, he became incapacitated from depression and migraine headaches. His eldest daughter, Patsy, helped rally his spirits and Jefferson once again gave his services to the new federal government, this time as Ambassador to France. Not only did he tend to diplomacy, but he also traveled throughout France and Italy eagerly taking notes on new inventions and agricultural techniques. Jefferson had never lost his boyhood respect for knowledge. He mastered architecture and incorporated European designs into his present plans for the new capitol building in Richmond, and later, for the University of Virginia. Ballooning, astronomy, smallpox vaccines, plants, animals—his range of inquiry was limitless. He transported Merino sheep, rice and cork back to America for farmers to use in experiments. He sketched plans for plows, drydocks and central heating systems. When he finally left Europe to join President George Washington's new cabinet as Secretary of State, Jefferson's belongings filled 86 huge crates. This new position would enable him to make one of his most enduring contributions to the new nation—the establishment of the American patent office.

Earlier he had successfully lobbied for a decimal system of coinage. In later years he would sell his huge personal library to the government and thus establish the Library of Congress. But included within his duties as Secretary of State, Jefferson provided the country with a solid basis to encourage creativity. Although he never patented any of his own inventions, such as the swivel chair, Jefferson believed an inventor should benefit from his originality. The first patent he granted was in 1790 to Samuel Hopkins of Vermont for a glassmaking process.

Left to tend to the patent office, Jefferson would have been supremely happy, but much of his attention had to be focused on foreign policy issues with England and France, as well as political disputes within the cabinet. Secretary of the Treasury Alexander Hamilton favored a strong central government which would center around the business community. One of Hamilton's supporters termed democracy "a dismal passport to a more wretched hereafter." Jefferson strongly disagreed with such a view and believed that a broad-based government would best serve the nation. Washington started to side more with Hamilton's viewpoint, and Jefferson, feeling increasingly isolated, resigned his post in December of 1793. This disagreement over political philosophy was to form the basis of the two-party system in American government.

When Jefferson returned to Monticello, he thought he was through with public life. He focused his attention on new farming techniques such as contour-plowing and crop-rotation. However, his increasing dissatisfaction with the federal government influenced him to once again seek elective office. He finished second in the presidential election of 1796, and thus served four years as Vice-President under John Adams. In 1800, Jefferson ran as a Democratic-Republican, and received the same number of electoral votes as Aaron Burr. The deadlocked election was thrown into the House of Representatives where 36 ballots were taken before Jefferson emerged victorious.

He served two terms as President, during which time he averted a near-war with England. In 1803 he presided over one of the greatest events in American history—the Louisianna Purchase. Seeking to secure access to the Mississippi River, an American delegation was instructed to purchase New Orleans from the French for two million dollars. Napoleon Bonaparte, who needed money to finance his European wars, decided to sell all 825,000 square miles for 15 million dollars. With no formal instructions to spend so much money, Robert Livingston and James Monroe nonetheless agreed to the deal. Jefferson had strong doubts about the constitutionality of the action, but it was approved by Congress in October, 1803.

The new land doubled the size of the United States, but it was a vast, unknown territory. To determine its potential, Jefferson in 1804 dispatched two Virginia neighbors, Meriwether Lewis and William Clark, on their famous expedition to the Pacific Ocean. The results of their journey delighted the President. He turned the White House into a veritable museum, laying out fossils on the East Room floor, hanging war bonnets from the walls, and letting two grizzly bear cubs roam around the lawn.

Jefferson never sought a third term. He morally opposed

the idea, and he also wanted the time to tend to a project dear to his heart—a state university for Virginia. In 1806 he had unsuccessfully proposed a national university to Congress. But by lobbying through the state legislature, a bill authorizing the University of Virginia was passed in 1818. He designed the buildings and personally oversaw construction through his telescope at nearby Monticello. Even though this incredible activity was taking place when he was in his seventies, Jefferson still had time to carefully work out a handicapping system, based on age, for his grandchildren's lawn races. When the nation found out that his charity and generosity had left him nearly penniless, citizens from Baltimore, New York and Philadelphia raised over 16 thousand dollars to aid him. Jefferson was overwhelmed by these gifts, and they allowed him to live in peace until his death on July 4, 1826—the fiftieth anniversary of the Declaration of Independence.

John Paul Jones

Stranded and penniless on the Island of Jamaica, the young, auburn-haired man desperately needed a job. Fortunately, luck smiled on him. The Irish actor, John Moody, hired him to perform in the play, *The Conscious Lovers.* History, however, would have remembered nothing of the young man's acting ability had he not occupied center stage 11 years later to shout the greatest response in naval history, "Struck, sir? No, I have just begun to fight."

A dreamer, poet and naval hero, John Paul Jones' life was touched by greatness and frustration. He was christened John Paul on July 6, 1747, in the Scottish fishing village of Arbigland. Not wishing to follow his father's trade of gardnening, he left home at 14 aboard the merchant brig, *Friendship.* After several voyages, John Paul became first mate of a slave ship. But the slave trade, with its death and foul conditions, took a heavy toll on his health and John Paul abandoned it at the age of 21. It was at this time he was forced to become an actor. But not for long. The love of the sea was strong within him, and John Paul soon captained his own ship, the *Betsy*.

While sailing her off the island of Tobago, a mutinous crew member attacked John Paul with a club. To protect himself, John Paul killed the man with a sabre stroke. When the crew's mood turned ugly, John Paul left the ship, added Jones to his name as a disguise, and left for America in 1773.

He scrimped around, lived on handouts from friends, and nearly paralyzed himself by introspective brooding. His life had no direction except for his interest in Freemasonry. Through lodge brothers he met some of the influential men of the period, including fellow redheads such as Thomas Jefferson and George Washington. Perhaps hair color sealed the bonds of Masonry, for nobody knows exactly how this unknown young Scotsman leaped from Virginia plantation life to the quarterdecks of the newly formed American Navy. When the Continental Congress released its officer slate, the 29-year-old Jones was listed as one of the five first-lieutenants.

Due to the incompetence of the officers senior to him, Jones received his own command. Several voyages distinguished his ability, but Jones became enmeshed in petty jealousies betwen his superiors and subordinates. Perhaps to the relief of both the Continental Congress and himself, Jones set sail for Europe in 1777 as captain of the 18-gun *Ranger*.

Jones carried to envoy Benjamin Franklin in France the news of Burgoyne's defeat at Saratoga. He also brought with him the radical idea of taking the war to the British by raiding their coast. To accomplish this task, Jones was to command the finest ship of the American fleet, the 40-gun *Indien*. Again, intrigue rose to plague him and he had to be content with the *Ranger*. Franklin's orders to Jones were simple, "Proceed with (your ship) in the manner you shall judge best for distressing the enemies of the United States, by sea or otherwise."

The captain used his free hand to raid English shipping and coastal towns, including the village of his birth. While on his raiding mission, Jones not only captured the 20-gun ship *Drake,* but he also drove up the price of shipping insurance, further adding to the cost of the British war effort. Jones should have received a triumphant welcome when he returned to France, but was instead blasted by accusations of incompetence. He was relieved of command of the *Ranger* and forced to pay his crew from his own pocket.

Shorebound, Jones' interests turned to Freemasonry and the ladies of the French Court. Through the influences of Masonic friends and the Duchess of Chartres, Jones received command of an old French warship called the *Duras.* Elated to be back at sea, Jones' first act was to rename the ship the *Bon Homme Richard* in honor of Benjamin Franklin.

Thus armed with a worn-out tub, a crew that mostly did not speak English, and guns that regularly misfired, Jones made naval history when he encountered the British *Serapis* on September 23, 1779.

As he closed for battle, the two other ships in his squadron promptly deserted the scene. Facing the more powerful British ship alone, Jones and his crew were undaunted. Laughter rang out after one sailor shouted, "Hold onto your pants, boys, here comes the 'Sea-raper!'" But the laughter was soon overwhelmed by cannon fire. Both ships broadsided each other so fiercely that gaping holes were blasted all the way through the decks. The carnage was aggravated when one of Jones' other ships returned and started to fire upon the *Bon Homme Richard* instead of the *Serapis.*

Jones realized that the only hope for victory lay in grappling the *Serapis* and fighting in hand-to-hand combat. By astonishing seamanship, Jones crossed the *Bon Homme Richard* in front of the*Serapis'* bow. Grabbing a rope and yelling, "I've got the son of a whore!" he lashed the two ships together while crew members blasted away with musket fire. It was during this struggle that Jones uttered his defiant "I have just begun to fight." After a grenade exploded in the *Serapis'* powder hold, the battle ended. His own ship, the *Bon Homme Richard,* was mauled so badly it sank the next day.

It was Jones' greatest, and last, triumph. Where the British failed to stop him at sea, politics and bureaucracy succeeded on land. He returned to America only to face new conflicts with a Congress that never reimbursed him for the money he was owed. Bitterly, he watched as the war passed him by.

When it ended, he traveled to Europe where the Russian Ambassador to France informed Jones that Empress Catherine II desired his services in fighting the Turks in the Black Sea. Intrigue, though, never seemed to escape him, and Jones soon found himself enmeshed in the same insubordinations and plots with the Russian leader, Potemkin, that had plagued him in the American navy. Although his strategies were effective, Jones was relieved of command. His Russian adventure shattered his nerves and health, and he returned to Paris where he died on July 18, 1792. Perhaps his soul was finally able to achieve in death what he claimed he wanted in life, "A life of poetic ease and quiet contemplation."

Emily Dickinson

The lives of some people resemble those of majestic trees. They stay physically rooted to one spot, yet they tower over their surroundings. They survey all that occurs on heaven and earth with a clear, sparkling vision denied to those less fortunate mortals who must stumble through the tangled thickets of the everyday landscape. Such was the life of the shy, gentle poet, Emily Dickinson, who for years never left her home. Yet she wrote poetry and verse of such exquisite beauty that total strangers sent her gifts in the mere hope of receiving a "thank-you" note.

Emily Dickinson's world-in-a-nutshell was the small town of Amherst, Massachusetts, where she was born into a prominent, well-to-do family on December 10, 1830. Her father was a lawyer, and also served as treasurer of Amherst College. He was a man whom she would come to greatly admire, while her mother would retain a less exciting, domestic role in Emily's life. Many of her early playmates were children of Amherst faculty members, along with an older brother, Austin, and a younger sister, Lavinia. In her later years, Emily's life centered around these family ties. She once wrote to her brother, "I think we miss each other more every day as we grow older, for we're most unlike everyone, and are therefore dependent on each other for delight."

Emily, however, did leave her family and home for a brief while at the age of 17 to attend Mount Holyoke Female Seminary, in South Hadley, Mass. She ended her studies in 1848, more because of an inability to adjust to the strict religious orthodoxy of the school than because of any intellectual shortcomings. Upon returning home, Emily began to develop reclusive tendencies. She once turned down an invitation to visit a friend by writing, "I'm afraid I've grown selfish in my dear home but I love it so, and when some pleasant friend invites me to spend a week with her, I look at my father and mother and Vinnie, and I say, 'No, no, I can't leave them, what if they die when I'm gone?'"

But while she disdained meeting people in public, she began writing what was to become a voluminous series of letters to close friends. Emily also had time for children, whom she viewed as co-conspirators against the adult world of respectability. Her niece, Martha Dickinson Bianchi, who was to later edit her verse, wrote that, "She lent a contraband thrill to the slightest pretext." Bianchi continued by writing, "It was here, (Emily's home) when 'Did' Jenkins and I set out to print in our own hand a little, neighborhood newspaper, we consulted Aunt Emily as to the name. She thought a minute, then answered decidedly, *The Fortnightly Bumble Bee,* promising us not only her subscription for all time, but contributions."

Following the death of her father in 1874 and her mother a year later, Emily spent most of her time either alone or with her sister Lavinia. Although they never quite under-

stood her, neighbors nonetheless viewed her with kindness and tolerance. She was called "the Myth" because of her retiring ways and her fondness for wearing white dresses which accented her slender figure and auburn hair. When one of Lavinia's friends came to the Dickinson house to play the piano, Emily remained half-hidden in the hall. As the recital ended, Emily sent out a poem on a silver tray.

Her poetry pumped throughout her soul as a lifeblood. Starting in 1862, Emily began to channel all of her inner energy into verse. She averaged a poem a day, producing nearly eighteen hundred which were bundled into neat packets and stored in a cherrywood dresser, where they lay hidden until after her death. In her solitude she experienced a zest for life that blossomed forth in works such as the following:

> I taste a liquor never brewed
> From tankards scooped in pearl
> Not all the vats upon the Rhine
> Yield such an alcohol.
>
> Inebriate of air am I
> and debauchee of dew,
> Reeling; through endless summer days
> From inns of molten blue.
>
> When landlords turn the drunken bee
> Out of the foxgloves door,
> When butterflies renounce their drams
> I shall but drink the more.
>
> Till seraphs swing their snowy hats
> And saints to windows run
> To see the little tippler
> Leaning against the sun.

From nature, Emily's thoughts also turned to the subjects of death and immortality. Her work dwelled upon the questions of what is death and what happens after death. Her attempts took her beyond the conventional theology of her time to a belief that all life is a quality of love and spirit that transcends time. For Emily Dickinson, the human being, as well as the poet, the question of death was a profound one, because the loss of loved ones affected her deeply. When Austin's son, her beloved nephew, Gilbert, died suddenly of typhoid fever at the age of eight in 1883, his death drained her own energy as well. She wrote to a friend in 1884, "I have not been strong for the last year.

The dyings have been too deep for me, and before I could raise my heart from one, another has come."

Her physical health was suffering, for unknown to but a few, Emily was slowly dying of the kidney disease of nephritis. A final coma enveloped her on May 11, 1886, and she died two days later. Only after her death did her family discover the extent of her poetry writing. In 1890, they published the treasures of her cherrywood dresser. Within her works were four simple lines that eloquently summed up the life of this quiet recluse:

> To fight aloud, is very brave
> But gallanter, I know
> Who charge within the bosom
> The cavalry of Wo.

Lizzie Borden

The poem convicted her, but the jury found her innocent. So stands the verdict in one of the most celebrated murder trials in American history. It had all the requirements of a great melodrama: unbearable family tensions, wealth and public position, gruesome savagery, famous lawyers, and most importantly, a beautiful woman, Lizbeth Andrews Borden.

Known to her friends as "Lizzie," she was born in 1860, the daughter of a prominent Falls River, Massachusetts, family. Her father, Andrew Borden, was a board member of several local banks and fabric mills. But although wealthy, he was not generous, least of all with love. Any chance for warmth and affection that Lizzie may have experienced ended when her mother died in 1862. Her father remarried two years later, but his new wife, Abby Durfee Gray Borden, never could fulfill the motherly needs of Lizzie or her older sister, Emma. As the years went on, an emotional powder keg built up in the Borden household. The tense peace that existed was based on a cold iciness that passed for cordiality.

The explosive situation ignited on the oppressively hot day of August 4, 1892. Mr. and Mrs. Borden had finished breakfast at 9:30 a.m. and their Irish maid, Bridget Sullivan, cleaned the table after them. Mr. Borden left the house to attend to downtown business while Mrs. Borden went upstairs. Lizzie was the only other person in the house with the two women, and when Mr. Borden returned at 10:40 a.m., Lizzie told him that Mrs. Borden had left the house to help a sick friend. Mr. Borden said he felt ill and went to take a nap on the living room couch. Lizzie chatted with Bridget for a while before the maid also went to take a nap. The city hall clock was ringing eleven o'clock when she lay down on her attic bed. Within 10 minutes she heard Lizzie cry out, "Maggie, come quick! Father's dead! Somebody's come and killed him."

Police were called and when they arrived at the scene they found Andrew Borden sprawled on the sofa with a bloody, bashed-in face, a severed nose and an eyesocket split in half. To their further horror, upstairs in the guest room they found Mrs. Borden's body also bludgeoned by upwards of 19 hatchet blows. But significantly, the blood on her body was dark and congealed, indicating she was murdered much earlier in the morning. Lizzie told the investigators she had gone to the barn on an errand and that she ran back to the house after she heard a groan and saw the screen door wide open. But when police checked the barn, they found no footprints had disturbed the dust on the floor. They also found a hatchet with a newly-broken handle hidden in a box of ashes in the house basement.

Because of the prestige of the Borden name, police were reluctant at first to arrest Lizzie, but then it became known that she tried to buy poisonous prussic acid the day before the murders. So, following an inquest and grand jury hearing, she was ordered to stand trial on June 5, 1893, in New Bedford, Mass.

The activity surrounding her trial can only be described as a circus. Western Union installed 30 extra telegraph lines to service the reporters who poured into town. The public hungered for gory details and the yellow journalists of the era did their best to provide them. For the most part, support rallied behind Lizzie. Few people wanted to believe the blue-eyed, red-haired woman actually murdered her parents. For instance, the president of the Women's Christian Temperance Union delivered an impassioned speech in which she harangued, "Is Lizzie Borden guilty? No, no, a thousand times no!"

But the prosecution tried to prove otherwise. District Attorney William Moody, who was trying his first murder case, offered into evidence the white, crushed skulls of the victims along with the testimony of police officers and Bridget Sullivan.

The prosecution was countered by a trio of defense lawyers that included former Massachusetts governor George D. Robinson. They tried to establish the basis for the mysterious assailant whom Lizzie claimed committed the crime. They pointed to arguments her father had had earlier with several men, along with establishing that there were strangers in the area. They also emphasized the fact that another unsolved axe-murder had occurred in the county five days before the trial began, and while Lizzie was still in jail. As for Lizzie, she never took the stand. Her only words during the entire 13-day trial were, "I am innocent. I leave it to my counsel to speak for me." Her counsel did exactly that. Robinson closed his case by saying, "Men of Bristol County, with hearts, with souls, men with rights who come from homes, firesides, wives and daughters, just as the little sparrow does not fall unnoticed to the ground, so Lizzie Borden is shielded by His Providence from above."

His closing argument, coupled with the trial judge's liberal instructions to the jury that damaged the prosecution's incriminating evidence, resulted in a verdict of innocent. Upon hearing the good news, Lizzie fainted and then murmured to her attorneys, "Take me home. I want to go to the old place tonight."

At first, the public and especially the women's movement rejoiced that she was found innocent. But as newspapers continued to bring more evidence to light, the mood turned and soon the following famous poem appeared:

> Lizzie Borden took an axe,
> and gave her mother 40 whacks.
> When she saw what she had done,
> She gave her father 41.

The public opinion had its effect on Lizzie. She moved with her sister to a fashionable house in Falls River and lived as a near-recluse for 34 years, spending much of her time watching birds and squirrels.

Upon her death on June 1, 1927, she bequeathed thirty thousand dollars to the Animal Rescue League of Falls River with the comment, "I have been fond of animals, and their need is great and there are so few who care for them."

Vincent Van Gogh

There was a genius in the man that defied description, so it was called madness. But in his madness and emotional torture, Vincent Van Gogh gave the world paintings that dance with colors so brilliant they force all who view them to question the way they look at the world.

Van Gogh began his short life on March 30, 1853. From the start, he was marked by tragedy—his parents had given him the name of an older son who had died a year earlier. As a youth, he was prone to temper-tantrums and fits of rage. These did not improve as he was sent to boarding school in an attempt to refine his abrupt behavior and unkempt dress. The only person who seemed to understand him was his younger brother, Theo, who was also a redhead. Theo knew Vincent was somehow special. It fell upon him, the task of not only encouraging Vincent, but also supporting him. Since their father, a poor Calvinist minister, could provide them with no future, the brothers were trained as art dealers by an uncle who had a successful gallery.

In 1873, Vincent was transferred to London, where he fell in love with his landlady's daughter. Rejected by her in a marriage proposal, he returned to Holland in a deep depression. His career also suffered. He was transferred to Paris and approached his work with a sullen contempt, refusing to sell any prints he personally did not like. This led to his dismissal in 1876.

A failure at both business and love, Van Gogh's life took a fanatical religious bent. He read the Bible constantly, and although Theo begged him to draw, Vincent instead sent him religious tracts. "Love God," he wrote, "All must be brought to His feet and I, unworthy, must bring them there; I must preach Christ crucified. I must live the Christ-life." After attending an evangelical school, Van Gogh sought to preach in the poorest district in Belgium—the Borinage. It was an Appalachia-type region where the people eked out a living mining coal. Van Gogh was appalled at the poverty he saw. Feeling that he could not justify even his small churchman's stipend, he gave it away. Van Gogh slept on the mud floor of a hut and lived on bread crusts. His frame grew gaunt and his eyes developed a wild, piercing glaze. Eventually the people of the district felt sorry for him. Church officials were so shocked at his appearance and behavior they forbade him to preach.

Van Gogh stayed in the Borinage for nine months, sleeping in haystacks and living on crumbs. The despair and physical privation were almost overwhelming. But during that period in 1879 a change occurred in his life. He broke with evangelism and started to find his direction as an artist. Anatomy books occupied his reading at night. In the daytime he sketched miners and weavers, feeling that their wearied faces mirrored the dignity of humanity.

Van Gogh returned to his family home in Etten when he was 28, but quarrels with his father and rejection of another marriage proposal proved too much to bear. He moved to the Hague where he soon began living with a pregnant prostitute named Sien. Although outraged by his brother's actions, Theo continued supporting him from his gallery earnings. Vincent began painting with water colors and for a while studied with the Dutch artist Mauve, until Mauve became disgusted by his behavior.

The Hague years were the turning point in Van Gogh's life, for now he began to think of himself as an artist. Love, however, was to deal him another disappointment. The warmth and tenderness he showed to Sien were rejected, and she left him to take up prostitution again. Van Gogh's ravaged emotions overflowed into painting. In August of 1881 he produced his first oil canvas, *Still Life With Jug.* He wrote to Theo, "I feel ideas about color coming to me as I paint which I never had before. They are big and exciting." He was his own teacher and his classroom was life. He painted the people and scenes of the Hague. After another stay with his parents, and wanderings that took him to Antwerp and the province of Neunen in Holland, Van Gogh arrived in Paris to live with his brother.

It was 1886. The Impressionist Movement was stirring the art world. Van Gogh finally found a group of men who agreed with his use of color. He enthusiastically set to work. Penniless as ever, he had to trade some of his 200 paintings to art dealer Pierre Tanguy in exchange for more paints. His subject material included portraits, still-lifes and cityscapes. The work of Japanese artists, with their delicate sense of line, also greatly influenced him at this time.

Paris during this period was an artist's dream, a dream, however, that Van Gogh could not handle. His rough personality grated on Theo, and Vincent was also tiring of Paris street life. He needed more light, more air, more color.

He intended to find these qualities in Marseilles, but stopped upon reaching the town of Arles in the south of France. The farm country was exploding into the spring of 1888. Van Gogh was so excited he could barely contain himself. "Nature here is so extraordinarily beautiful," he wrote to Theo. "It's the chance of a lifetime. I feel a different man from the one who came here—I let myself go, paint what I see and how I feel and hang the rules." It was all his hand could do to keep up with the pace of his vision. He painted *Summer Evening,* a three square foot canvas, at one sitting.

Van Gogh's work was vitally alive, but his physical vitality was suffering. Whatever money from Theo which was not spent on supplies was squandered on absinthe. Van Gogh's mind, which was never quite stable, was becoming unglued. The painter Paul Gaugin came to live with him in November of 1888 and for a while cared for Van Gogh's physical needs.

Van Gogh idolized his friend, but even this love did not last long. The two had a falling-out over a prostitute who preferred Gaugin. Jealous, Van Gogh threatened him with a razor, and then turned it on himself, hacking off a slice of his right ear.

In an attempt to stabilize his mind, Vincent went to the mental institution at St. Remy, but the stay did him no good. Despondent over his lack of acceptance by the art world, and tired of the suffering he brought to himself and others, Vincent Van Gogh shot himself on July 29, 1890.

Theo collapsed at his graveside. Having lost Vincent, he was a broken man. Theo returned to the Netherlands from Paris, but died from a stroke six months later. The two are buried together at a cemetery in the Netherlands.

One of Van Gogh's biographers said of him, "He does not seem to have owed to any individual the release of the extremely rare gifts he possessed and the opportunities to apply them. For Vincent might just as easily have become a thinker, hero, poet or saint as a painter."

In fact, he may have been all of these at once.

Sarah Bernhardt

"There are five kinds of actresses," Mark Twain once said, "Bad actresses, fair actresses, good actresses, great actresses and Sarah Bernhardt."

Twain was right in putting Sarah Bernhardt in a class by herself. While the first four groups of actresses acted upon a stage of wood, Sarah's stage was the whole world. She was the greatest actress of her time, and perhaps all time. In the course of her colorful 61-year career, her genius and beauty brought audiences to their feet and lovers to their knees.

As one critic said, "She could enter a convent, discover the North Pole, kill an emperor or marry a Negro king and it would not surprise me. She is not an individual but a complex of individuals." What makes this comment so true is that at one time, Sarah actually did want to enter a convent.

She was born October 23, 1844, the daughter of a law student and a Jewish Dutch courtesan. From the beginning, Sarah's frail health made it doubtful if she would live past 20. She hardly knew her father, and her mother spent little time with her. Yet she saw to it that Sarah was baptized and placed in a convent school when she was 12 years old. The young girl soon became a religious fanatic and wanted to devote her life to the Church as a nun. When asked about her future, Sarah said, "I shall marry God."

But such determination did not impress her mother. She decided Sarah needed a career. Her influential friend, the Duc de Morny, happened to be present during one of Sarah's passionate outbursts of temper. To him goes the credit of observing, "The girl's a born actress. She ought to be sent to the Conservatoire for training." Sarah totally opposed the idea until she saw a performance of the Theatre Francaise and experienced its magic. As she later wrote in her *Memoirs,* "It was the curtain of my life which was rising."

She had to audition to be admitted to the Conservatoire. The shy 15-year-old was extremely nervous when she mounted the platform to give a rendition of a fable called *Les Deux Pigeons* by La Fontaine. Facing the judges, Sarah delivered her lines to this, her first audience. They, like thousands to follow, loved her.

Her career, however, was not to know instant success. After studying several years at the Conservatoire, Sarah received a few small roles at the Theatre Francaise. It seemed that Sarah's career would fizzle before it even started. One reviewer wrote of her acting, "The fact that Mademoiselle Bernhardt is inadequate is not very important. She is making her debut, and it is perfectly natural that among these beginners there should be some who do not succeed. Many must be tried before a good one is found." Sarah became so despondent she thought of committing suicide by drinking liquid rouge.

But the world was not yet ready to lose her. At 19, Sarah was strikingly-radiant with a thin figure, blue eyes and a frizzy, reddish mane of hair. She attracted as one of her lovers a Belgian prince by whom she bore a child, Maurice, when she was barely 20. The prince asked her to marry him if only she would leave the theatre. Sarah refused. Solely on her own, with a child to support, Sarah knew she needed to devote herself with renewed fervor to acting. Her maternal instincts thus helped supply her with the determination she needed to succeed.

Sarah managed to wangle a job at a more experimental state theatre, the Odeon, and it was here that her career skyrocketed. She performed as a page boy in a play called *Le Passant* in 1869, which played for over 100 nights and brought her admirers ranging from author Alexandre Dumas to Emperor Napoleon Bonaparte III.

Sarah played at the Odeon to ever-increasing audiences until the Franco-Prussian War in 1870. Rather than leave Paris as the German armies approached, Sarah converted the Odeon into a field hospital and made herself chief nurse. Sarah used all of her charm and connections to stock

the hospital. The joke around Paris was "Don't go near the Odeon in any warm clothes. Sarah Bernhardt will rip them off your backs for her soldiers!"

When peace returned, Sarah again starred at the Odeon, starting in October, 1871. Ironically, her leading man was one of her former patients. Sarah's career never again faltered. Her best roles were in classical drama, and she delivered her lines in a voice that one reviewer described as being "more than gold, there was thunder and lightning, there was heaven and hell."

Despite recurring poor health, Sarah devoted boundless energy to her work, often starting her day at 3 a.m. Curiously, throughout her career, Sarah never got over stage fright and at times had to be pushed onto the stage.

By 1880, her fame had become so great she was offered the fabulous sum of one thousand dollars a performance to tour America. Her landing in New York was an extravaganza. When one reporter said, "New York didn't give Dom Pedro of Brazil such an ovation," Sarah drily observed, "Yes, but he was only an emperor."

The first American tour was followed by seven others, in addition to world tours which took Sarah and her company to Australia, Madagascar and Sough America. So adoring were the crowds that jewels were thrown to her on stage, and men spread their coats before her so that she would not have to tread on dusty sidewalks.

In her later years, Sarah not only acted, but also directed and managed her own stage company which played at the Theatre Sarah Bernhardt. Her devotion to work continued even after doctors amputated her right leg in 1916. In fact, it was at this point that Sarah decided to start acting in motion pictures.

Had she just been known for her theatrical ability, Sarah's fame would have been secured for posterity. But the amount of coverage devoted to her eccentricities and romances was even greater than that showered on her acting. Early in her life, Sarah acquired a rosewood coffin after doctors told her that she had little more than a few months to live. She outlived their predictions, but nevertheless kept the coffin with her on all of her tours. She often slept in it and used it as a table upon which to serve tea.

Her world tours often were scheduled in order to pay back debts incurred by extravagant spending, such as boarding a pet lion at her summer house. Much has been made of her love life, but Sarah also counted as close friends some of the leading figures of the day, men such as Thomas Edison and King Edward VII of England. Perhaps she got along so well with people because she remained unaffected by fame. She delighted in practical jokes, such as autographing pictures to total strangers with the phrase, "To the most important person in my life."

When Sarah Bernhardt died on March 26, 1923, nearly a million people watched the funeral procession. In their hearts was the tribute once paid to her by critic Francisque Sarcey, "She is unique and no one will ever take her place."

Mark Twain

Try this. Ask the next person you are talking with to name an American author. Even if he has never read a book in his life, chances are he will say Mark Twain, the pen name of Sam Clemens. In a lifetime that began with the appearance of Haley's Comet on November 30, 1835, and ended when the comet returned on April 21, 1910, Mark Twain became the most widely respected author this country has ever produced, not to mention his other careers as riverboat pilot, silver miner, newspaper reporter, businessman, publisher, lecturer and world traveler. He was both the recorder and the embodiment of the American Experience.

Samuel Langhorne Clemens was born within earshot of boatmen calling out his future pen name, "Mark Twain," which meant two fathoms of water and safe passage for the riverboats which glided past the small Mississippi River town of Florida, Missouri. Twain's father was a storekeeper. When his business failed, he moved the family to the slightly larger town of Hannibal, where the townspeople elected him Justice of the Peace. Even at an early age, Twain's curly red hair and twinkling blue eyes made him stand out among his friends; boys such as Tom Blankenship, who lived with his drunken father in a dilapidated old shack and who could skip school to hunt or fish whenever he liked. Twain was not so fortunate. At the age of 13, he was apprenticed to a local printer, and he pursued that trade in a half-hearted manner even though his older brother, Orion, hired him to work on the newspaper he published in Hannibal. The river was what he wanted—the river with its dandies, gamblers, elegant ladies, strapping black boiler stokers, proud captains, grandeur, excitement and endless flow of life.

He got his wish when at the age of 21, and penniless in New Orleans, he managed to persuade the dean of the riverboat pilots, Horace Bixby, to take him on as a cub pilot. Twain learned the Mississippi well, and was soon one of the river's youngest pilots. He earned the princely sum of two hundred fifty dollars a month and dressed himself in patent leather shoes, bow ties and starched white shirts. He mastered the grandest job on the river, and his life held nothing but promise, when, on an up-river run to St. Louis in 1861, a warning shot was fired across his bow. The Civil War had begun. An Era had ended.

> Territorial Governors . . . are nothing but politicians who go to the outskirts of countries and suffer the privations there to build up stakes and come back U.S. Senators.

Following a short stint in the Confederate Army which he later wrote about in the story *A Private History of a Campaign that Failed,* Twain traveled westward as an assistant to Orion, who had been appointed as secretary for the governor of the Nevada Territory. Twain soon neglected his slim duties and set out to make a fortune as a silver miner. After enduring snowstorms, floods and hours of shoveling worthless tons of rock, Twain decided the life of a miner was a bit too strenuous for his self-admitted lazy disposition. He sold his pick and shovel and walked 130

miles to Virginia City where he was offered a job as a reporter on the *Territorial Enterprise* for twenty five dollars a week. He soon evolved the habit of neglecting straight news to write outrageous fiction, such as the story of miners finding a 300-year-old petrified man whose fossilized hand was thumbing his nose. At this time Twain also began using his soon-to-be-famous pen name, which readers were eagerly associating with his hilarious columns about human shortcomings. Twain eventually left Virginia City and worked for several other Western papers, including the San Francisco *Morning Call.* In San Francisco, Twain met writer Bret Harte, who encouraged him to record some of the stories he heard in the mining camps. Following a five-month trip to the Hawaiian Islands in 1866, Twain penned, "Well, I called on good-natured, garrulous old Simon Wheeler, and I inquired after your friend, Leonidas W. Smiley, as you requested me to do, and I hereunto append the result . . ."

The resulting tale was *The Celebrated Jumping Frog of Calaveras County,* which is now considered a classic of American literature.

> The gentle reader will never, never know what a consumate ass he can become until he goes abroad.

Twain combined his Hawaiian adventures into a series of highly successful lectures. his following in the West was becoming sizeable, so he approached the Alta *Californian* about sponsoring an excursion to Europe on the ship, *Quaker City,* in return for the dispatches he would send back. His wildly funny observations created a sensation when they were printed. Upon his return in 1867, he combined them into his first money-making success, *Innocents Abroad.* Not only did his trip bring him fame, it also brought him a wife.

> I have really no intention to do anything except court Livy.

Charles Langdon, a friend of Twain's on the *Quaker City* had shown him a picture of his 22-year-old sister, Olivia, who was known to her family as "Livy." Twain thought she was beautiful, and fell in love with her even before they met. His mind was already set on marriage, but Livy was shocked by his rough manners, swearing and cigar smoking. He neglected his profitable lecturing career to spend more time with her, and after much persuasion, she agreed to marry him. Their wedding on February 2, 1870, started a love affair that would last for the rest of their lives. Twain's popularity as a writer continued to climb as he capitalized on recounting his younger days in such books as *Roughing It* (1872), which told about his silver mining escapades, and *Tom Sawyer* (1876), about his boyhood in Hannibal. After living for a brief while in Hartford, Conneticut, the family, which now included two of eventually three daughters, moved in 1872 to Elmira, New York. Twain secluded himself in a study designed to resemble a Mississippi River boat pilot-house and worked from morning to late afternoon, at which time he set aside his typewriter and told his daughters yarns about cats named Calitne, Catasqua and Cattauragus. Mark Twain liked cats as much as he did cigars.

In 1876, he began to work on a sequel to *Tom Sawyer* by drawing on his memories of Tom Blankenship and his Hannibal days. He puttered sporadically with the project for the next eight years. Of the eventual result, Ernest Hemingway was to comment, "All modern American literature comes from one book by Mark Twain called *Huckleberry Finn.*"

A man with a new idea is a Crank, until the idea succeeds.

Had Twain stayed with writing, his steady success would have been assured. But he was forever investing in half-baked inventions that drained his capital and energy. One, the Paige Typesetter, swallowed three hundred thousand dollars of his money and, along with the failure of his publishing house, helped drive him into bankruptcy. To pay off his creditors, Twain left on a world-wide lecture tour and an extended stay abroad from which he gathered the material for the book, *Following the Equator,* which was printed in 1897. While he was overseas, one of his daughters died of meningitis. Twain was heartbroken and lapsed into a black grief which he never quite overcame.

Following Livy's death in 1904, his sadness reflected itself in a period of cynical, ascerbic writing which included such works as *The Man Who Corrupted Hadleyburg* and *Letters from the Earth.* Although remorseful, he nonetheless ventured into public life, making appearances before Congress to lobby for improved copyright laws and travelling to England to receive an honorary degree from Oxford University. His last years were spent working on his autobiography, for Twain knew his time was limited. Haley's Comet was due to return, and when it did, Twain suffered a heart attack and lapsed into a fatal coma. His last words were simply, "Goodbye."

Margaret Sanger

Rather than be hauled away in a patrol wagon, the small, gray-eyed, red-haired woman walked a mile to the Raymond Street Jail in New York City, where she spent the night in a roach-infested, grimy cell before being released on bail the next morning. Her crime? Offending the morals of the people of New York State by providing information on contraception. Her name? Margaret Sanger—the woman who made the phrase "birth control" part of the English language. Viewed as a saint by tens of thousands of women, and condemned as an affront to decency by the Catholic Church and the U.S. Post Office, Margaret Sanger was one of the most controversial figures in America during the early years of the 20th century. This is strange, since in her words, all she really wanted to do was uphold the dignity of life. "The first right of every child," she said, "is to be wanted, to be desired, to be planned with an intensity of love that gives it its title to being."

The eventual course of her life's work was to have its roots in her early childhood. She was born September 14, 1879, in Corning, New York, the sixth of eleven children of a poor Irish family. From her father, Michael Higgins, she inherited a social consciousness. He carved gravestones for a living but was more content being the town radical and an early backer of the Socialist Party. Margaret saw in her mother, Anne, the effects of too many children and too little money. She was wracked by tuberculosis, the disease that was to claim her life in 1896. Margaret was to spend much time nursing her mother. From this experience she drew the determination to attend nursing school in New York City, which she did in 1902.

While in school, she met a young architect, Bill Sanger, whom she married when she was 23. A child soon followed and their marriage was a happy one. But tuberculosis struck Margaret and she had to leave the city for health reasons.

The family moved to Hastings-on-the-Hudson where Margaret had two more children and fought off a bout of deep depression brought on by her illness and a feeling that she lacked purpose in the quiet of country life. Margaret's health eventually recovered to the point that, when her husband accepted a commission in New Jersey, she was only too willing to move the family back to New York City. The Sanger household in 1912 soon became involved in the current of radical ideas that was sweeping the country. Margaret eagerly joined with her husband in entering Socialist politics, and they became friends with such figures as political leader Eugene Debs, journalist John Reed, and anarchist Emma Goldman.

It was in this electrically charged political climate that Margaret took her first steps along her life's path. She reluctantly agreed to fill in one night as a speaker at a women's assembly. Not knowing what else to talk about, she drew upon her nursing background and spoke on childbirth and family health. The speech was so popular that she began writing a series of articles in the Socialist newspaper entitled, "What Every Girl Should Know." Thousands of issues were sold, but the subject matter so startled the official post office censor, Anthony Comstock, that he threatened to revoke the newspaper's mailing rights if a scheduled article on syphilis appeared. Comstock's power as judge and jury could have put the newspaper out of business. It retaliated by printing a page entirely blank except for the words:

What Every Girl Should Know

NOTHING!

By order of the Post Office Department

This stifling censorship came close on the heels of a profoundly wrenching experience Margaret had as a nurse. She had tried to save the life of a woman, Sadie Sachs, who was dying from a self-induced abortion. But she was too late. As Margaret left the small apartment, all she could remember were the dead woman's husband wailing, "My God! My God!", and the words of the doctor who, when asked by Sadie how she could prevent another pregnancy, chuckled, "Tell your husband to sleep on the roof." There was no turning back. She had found her calling.

Margaret began combing libraries for contraception information, but all the books were hopelessly out of date. Because of its stuffy moral codes, the United States was decades behind the work being done in Europe. So in 1913, the Sangers left for France, where Margaret could pursue her research and Bill could begin his long-desired career as a painter. While abroad, Bill and Margaret succumbed to the pulling forces of different careers and parted company. Bill remained in Paris for several years while Margaret returned to New York with their children. For all intents, it was the end of their marriage, and it would be eight years before she would remarry.

Upon returning home, Margaret championed the feminist cause by coining the phrase "birth control" and starting the National Birth Control League. She also started publishing a newspaper entitled *The Woman Rebel*, in which she maintained "a woman's body belongs to herself alone!" She was soon indicted on nine felony counts for sending obscenity through the mails. Stubbornly, she would not compromise on a bargained sentence because of

her principles. Rather than face almost certain conviction and a possible 45-year prison sentence, Margaret jumped bail and exiled herself to England in 1914. While abroad she began what was to become a lifelong friendship with British sex researcher Havelock Ellis, and she also visited Holland where she was impressed by the Dutch system of birth control clinics.

The thoughts of home, however, still gnawed at her. She returned to America in 1915 and surrendered herself to authorities. Luckily, the mood of the country had changed. Birth control had come into the open and influential citizens began flocking to her cause. When Margaret decided to defend herself, the government dropped its charges rather than risk embarassment. It was a triumph for Margaret. She followed it up by a nationwide speaking tour which at times had to overcome interference from the Catholic Church in the scheduling of lectures.

Birth control leagues began springing up all over the country, but she felt it was not enough. A clinic was needed similar to the Dutch model to show women how to go about practicing birth control. Margaret and her sister, Ethel, a registered nurse, rented a storefront in Brooklyn and printed up several hundred leaflets which read:

> Mothers! Can you afford to have a large family?
>
> If not, why do you have them?
>
> Safe, harmless information can be obtained
> from trained nurses.

The clinic opened October 16, 1916, and over 140 women came the first day. The second day, Margaret was arrested by the vice-squad and led off to the Raymond Street Jail. At issue was a New York State law that said nobody could give out contraceptive information except doctors. This was always interpreted to benefit men seeking facts on how to stop venereal disease. At her trial on January 29, 1917, the three judges hearing her case were emotionally touched by the long train of poor mothers who testified to the help Margaret offered. They extended leniency to Margaret if she would agree not to violate the law again. After a long silence, she answered, "I cannot promise to obey a law I do not respect." For her courageous stand, she spent 30 days in the Blackwells Island Jail, where she wasted little time in establishing an education program for the women in her cell block. When she was released, hundreds of her supporters greeted her by singing *The Marseillaise.* The courts, however, had not written the final word in her case. Upon appeal, the New York Court of Appeals ruled that disease meant a disorder in the body. Since pregnancy fell under that classification, doctors were allowed to give birth control advice to a woman to protect her health. This circumspect ruling was a far cry from the total freedom Margaret had fought for, but at least a door had opened.

The rest of her life, until she died of a heart attack on September 6, 1966, was devoted to the cause of birth control and human rights. She cheerfully spent many long hours in speaking, writing and organizing. Because of her efforts, the first Conference on World Population was held in Geneva in 1927. She lived to see the movement, which started as an illegal subject of conversation, expand into the International Planned Parenthood Foundation. As for Margaret, the jail cells were transformed into reception halls as she was honored by world leaders and nominated for the Nobel Peace Prize.

In 50 years, Margaret Sanger helped change the world by believing in both a cause and herself. "Life has taught me one supreme lesson," she wrote. "This is that we must—if we are to live at all—put our convictions into action."

Vladimir Lenin

On March 31, 1917, a very special train pulled out of the railroad yards in Zurich, Switzerland. No questions were asked of the 30 passengers—all Russian political exiles. No baggage was inspected. No passports were checked. When everyone was aboard, the doors of the train were sealed. Within a small sleeping compartment of this train sat a short, balding man with a red fringe of hair, pointed beard and piercing eyes—Vladimir Ilyich Lenin. Years later Winston Churchill was to comment, "The Germans transported Lenin in a sealed train like a plague-bacillus from Switzerland to Russia." The analogy was an appropriate one. For Lenin carried with him the germ of an idea, an idea that was to evolve through the bloodshed of revolution into the modern Soviet State.

The Russia into which Lenin was born on April 22, 1870, was a backward, agrarian nation dominated by the Tsar, a corrupt officialdom and the Russian Orthodox Church. Fortunately for Lenin, he was spared from the massive illiteracy that existed in rural areas. His father was a school superintendant who infused his family with a love of books, learning and a concern for those less fortunate in life.

His older brother, Alexander, took this concern with him when he left to study biology at the University of St. Petersburg. Soon he was radicalized by the crushing poverty extant in the city and fell in with a group of students who felt the only way to bring about change in Russia was to assassinate the Tsar. Police, however, discovered the plot, and in 1887 Alexander was executed for his involvement. Alexander's death was to have a far-reaching effect, for when Lenin soon afterward attended Kazan University, he was expelled for attending a student protest meeting. The secret police were fearful that Alexander's ideas had tainted his younger brother. They certainly had. While out of school, Lenin began reading the works of Karl Marx, and started to develop revolutionary tendencies of his own. He also began to independently study for the law exam, and after passing it with honors, moved to St. Petersburg in 1893 to set up a practice.

But a lawyer's life soon gave way to preaching of insurrection. Disguising himself as a workman, Lenin entered the factories in the city to tell the workers about Marxism. He was soon arrested and thrown into prison for a year, where he occupied himself by doing fingertip-pushups and other calisthenics to strengthen his body. Following inprisonment, he was sentenced to Siberia from 1896 to 1899. What could have proven to be a bleak exile was lessened by the presence of Nadezhda Krupskaya, a fellow revolutionary whom Lenin knew in St. Petersburg. The two were married, and for the rest of her life Nadezhda served as a loving companion and a devoted supporter of her husband.

After being released, Lenin again plunged into revolutionary work. When Russia proved too dangerous a place to live, he and Nazezhda moved; first to Germany, and then to London in 1902. He tirelessly set about building a party-structure by contacting other revolutionaries, such as exiled Leon Trotsky, while at the same time setting down his views on revolution in newspaper articles and in the book, *What Is to Be Done?* This was a handbook of tactics in which Lenin advocated leadership by a small band of professionals so as to lessen group dissension. Lenin took these ideas to the Second Congress of the Russian Social-Democratic Labour Party in 1903, where delegates accepted *What Is to Be Done?* as the party handbook. At the London meeting, those favoring revolution were in the majority, so they were called the Bolsheviks, after the Russian word "bolshoi" meaning big. Those in the minority, who favored change by peaceful means, were called the Mensheviks, after the Russian word "menshie," meaning less.

Left on their own, the exiled radicals would have spent endless meetings debating arcane theories. Meanwhile, events were moving quickly in Russia, making revolution seem totally feasible. Famine was sweeping the land, and in January, 1905, a crowd of two hundred thousand workers carrying religious icons and pictures of the Tsar appeared peacefully before the Winter Palace in St. Petersburg to ask for more bread. Tsar Nicholas II had left St. Petersburg rather than meet the workers, and the Cossack guards that remained fired on the marchers, killing dozens and embittering thousands. A general strike followed. The crew of the battleship *Potemkin* mutinied, and workers in Moscow fought government troops from barricades until they were decimated by artillery barrages. Lenin, meanwhile, was in Geneva, and he immediately advocated an armed uprising. He wrote to leaders in Russia, "It requires furious energy and more energy . . . For Christ's sake throw out all your schemes, consign all rights and privileges to the devil. If the Fighting Organization does not have at least two or three hundred squads in Petersburg in one or two months, then it is a dead committee and should be buried."

Lenin's words proved prophetic, for the revolution fizzled due to lack of direction after the Tsar agreed to several concessions, such as the formation of a parliament (the Duma) and amnesty for political exiles. Lenin returned to Russia where he agitated against the Duma, which he regarded as a worthless sellout. When an informer betrayed a Bolshevik document advocating revolution, police closed in and Lenin had to flee for his life to Finland. The ensuing years, from 1907 to 1917, were hard ones. Lenin and Nadezhda moved throughout Europe, and were always in a state of near-poverty, supported mostly by money from his family, and bank holdups staged by other Bolsheviks such as Joseph Stalin. He was suffering from doubts and pessimisim, and nearly succumbed to a nervous breakdown in 1912. While in Geneva, he remarked to his wife, "I feel as if I have come here to be buried."

But he never stopped. During all the years of lonely exile Lenin constantly studied and preached the teachings of Marx as he interpreted them to be best for Russia. One of his contemporaries said of him, "There is no other man who thinks and dreams of revolution—twenty-four hours a day." When World War I broke out in 1914, Lenin was beside himself with joy. He knew it was the beginning of the end. "Take your rifles and turn them against your officers and the capitalists!" he wrote. Lenin hardly needed to radicalize the soldiers. After several disastrous defeats, Russian troops deserted in droves and, coupled with food shortages at home, the nation teetered towards chaos.

Tsar Nicholas II, an ineffectual ruler at best, could not contain the rebellion. He was arrested in March, 1917, and the Duma formed a provisional government to take his place. Although most people were sick of the war, this government wanted to continue it, mostly because loans of money from the Allies kept it in power. The German High Command, however, wanted Russia out of the war so that it could concentrate its troops on the Western Front.

Since the Bolsheviks were advocating peace, German intelligence officers thought it wise to offer Lenin transport across Germany to the Russian frontier. Lenin felt it might be a setup to murder him, but it was a chance he had to take. He arrived in St. Petersburg (renamed Petrograd, and still later Leningrad) on April 3, 1917, and immediately began marshalling his party. Lenin had been abroad so long that few Russians knew who he was. But he was soon elecrifying the crowds with his speeches. "We were presented with a blazing, dazzling exotic beacon . . . a note not discordant, but novel, harsh, somewhat stunning," wrote a Russian historian on the scene.

Lenin was not going to let this opportunity slip through his fingers. He was more ruthless and completely dedicated than any other Russian political leader, and he confidently moved into the power vacuums caused by their indecisiveness. On October 25, 1917, thirty-four weeks after Lenin entered the country, a Bolshevik coup toppled the Provisional Government of Alexander Kerensky. A thunderous ovation greeted Lenin as he rose to address the

troops and workers at the Winter Palace in Petrograd. He thundered, "We should now occupy ourselves in Russia in building up a proletarian Socialist state. Long live the world-wide Socialist Revolution."

Many men in history have fomented a revolution, but few have remained in power long afterward. Lenin was the exception. He swiftly moved to consolidate his hold on the government by outlawing the newly-elected assembly and using a secret police force, known as the Cheka, to silence dissidents. One of his most important tasks was to conclude a peace with Germany, which he did in March, 1918. Although the terms were harsh, Lenin was able to now use his armies to fight in the civil war that was raging against his Bolshevik regime. His opponents nearly assassinated him on August 1, 1918. Finally, in 1921, Red armies under the leadership of Leon Trotsky succeeded in controlling the country. But there was no time for rest. Food shortages, brought on by constant warfare and a drought, were again crippling Russia. This was coupled with abysmally poor production in the state-controlled factories where the workers also served as managers. Lenin's hope for a worldwide socialist revolution never materialized and he was thus forced to deal with the hated capitalist countries. Always a pragmatist, Lenin altered his economic philosophy and signed trade agreements to develop Russian resources, and he also sought relief-aid from the United States.

The years of relentless struggle, however, took their toll on Lenin. He suffered a series of strokes and gradually let others take over the Party. In his weakened state, he was unable to prevent Stalin from achieving total control. Lenin wrote of Stalin, "Comrade Stalin has concentrated enormous power in his hands, and I am not sure he always knows how to use that power with sufficient caution." His words went unheeded, and when the final stroke occurred on January 21, 1924, thousands braved -30 degree weather to view his funeral procession. Millions more have paid their respects as they pass by his body which lies in a mausoleum in the Moscow Kremlin, a memorial to a man whose will and ambition forged a country.

Winston Churchill

World War II has left us with the legacy of nuclear weapons, jet aircraft and intercontinental missiles. All of these massive, destructive tools obscure the fact that the most powerful weapon of World War II was the English language, and its greatest tactician was Winston Spencer Churchill. With powerful genius, he marshalled simple nouns and verbs into speeches that trumpeted across a bomb-shattered land and inspired courage and hope in the hearts of his beleaguered countrymen. During the terribly dark days of the Battle of Britain, Winston Churchill and the English people shared their Finest Hour.

It was an hour that took a lifetime in making, and an hour that almost never chimed, for as a youth, Churchill was looked upon as an almost hopeless dolt. He was born November 30, 1874, with the silver spoon of wealth in his mouth. His father, Lord Randolph Churchill, was cutting a distinguished path in British politics and his mother, Jennie, an American heiress, was a focal point of aristocratic social life. With all of their interest directed outward, neither parent had much time for their son. Churchill lived through a frustrating, rebellious childhood that saw him almost continually at the bottom of his class at school. His main source of happiness came from playing with his collection of several hundred toy soldiers.

Taking notice of this hobby, his father suggested he pursue a military career. Winston was enthusiastic about the idea; after three attempts he finally passed the entrance exam for the Sandhurst Military Academy. The experience marked a turning point in his life, for Churchill now excelled at his studies and eagerly read the philosophy and history he found so distasteful in public school. After graduating eighth in a class of 250, he served in the Sudan, India, and also as an observer in the Spanish-American War in Cuba, a period during which he formed a lifelong taste for cigars.

His military training, along with some articles he had written while in India, formed the perfect background for him to serve as a war correspondent during the Boer War against the Dutch in South Africa. Leaving England in September, 1899, he was captured two months later and imprisoned.

Rather than submit to this disgrace, Churchill wrote a farewell letter to his captors and escaped at night over the prison wall. Not knowing a word of Dutch, and suffering from hunger and exhaustion, he almost miraculously sought help at the only English-sympathizing house in a 30-mile radius. The Boers had issued a dead-or-alive reward for Churchill that described him as "about five feet eight inches tall, walks with a forward stoop, red-brownish hair, small moustache, talks through his nose and cannot pronounce the letter "S" correctly." After hiding two days in a rat-infested mine shaft, Churchill was smuggled out of the country and hailed as a hero when he returned to England.

He capitalized on his fame by getting elected to Parliament in 1900, thus beginning a career that would not culminate until he had become the greatest statesman of the modern era. But fame requires a price, and Churchill soon acquired enemies who bridled at his personal ambition. Even his marriage to Clementine Hozier in 1908, and the several children that followed, did not diminish his drive, and he moved up the political ladder until he was named First Lord of the Admiralty in 1911.

Churchill threw himself wholeheartedly into his new task, even learning to fly so as to fully appreciate the value of the airplane in warfare. Largely due to his concentrated energy, the Royal Navy was in superb condition when Britain entered World War I in 1914. As top naval man in a maritime nation, Churchill was one of England's most important leaders. He put forward the plan to invade Turkey through the Dardenelles and thus pressure Germany on a third front. The Gallipoli campaign in 1915 proved a ghastly fiasco since it was not properly executed. Over a quarter of a million British troops were killed or wounded, and Churchill was forced to resign from the Admiralty. In a deep depression, he told a friend, "I am finished." To vent his energy, he took up painting, but this proved too mild an undertaking while a war was being fought. He enlisted in the army and served in France as a battalion commander, but was soon recalled to Parliament to finish out the war as Minister of Munitions. Following the armistice in 1918, sentiment turned against Churchill and his party. Suffering from appendicitis during the 1922 election, he lost in a landslide to Edwin Scrymgeour, a Prohibitionist. "In the twinkling of an eye," said Churchill, "I found myself without an office, without a seat, without a Party and without an appendix."

Fortunately, he retained his sense of humor. When he retired to his country estate of Chartwell, Churchill busied himself with painting, writing and his new-found hobby of bricklaying. He didn't have a chance to build many walls, for in 1924, Churchill was re-elected to Parliament and appointed Chancellor of the Exchequer, a position held by his father 38 years earlier. As a financial leader, Churchill was a distinct failure and some of his policies severely undermined British trade. He also could not empathize with the plight of British workers, especially the coal miners. The mine owners were going to cut wages and lengthen hours, and in protest the miners went on strike. They were joined by a million and a half other workers in a sympathy gesture. To combat the strike, Churchill hammered away at the unions through a newspaper he edited. The strike ended after 10 days in May of 1926, but British workers remained bitter towards Churchill until the start of World War II.

The next several years saw Churchill removed from the center of power, but he certainly was not idle. He continued with his writing career and also began speaking against the rising threat of Germany. He warned, "All these bands of sturdy Teutonic youths with the light of desire in their eyes to suffer for their Fatherland are not looking for status—they are looking for weapons."

In criticizing Britain's unpreparedness he railled, "It is much better to be frightened now than to be killed hereafter." But his colleagues would not listen. They supported a policy of appeasement that encouraged German military boldness which culminated when Adolf Hitler invaded Poland on September 1, 1939. The German armies appeared invincible. They rolled over Western Europe and only stopped when they reached the English Channel. They would go no further, for in England, the newly appointed Prime Minister was breathing fire into his people with such immortal words as, "I have nothing to offer but blood, toil, tears and sweat . . . You ask, what is our aim? I can answer in one word: It is victory, victory at all costs, victory in spite of all terror, victory, however long and hard the road may be; for without victory, there is no survival."

For the next six years, Churchill became a human dynamo who directed his attention to everything from chocolate rations to the invasion of Europe. With President Franklin D. Roosevelt, he drew up the Atlantic Charter setting out the principles of free nations, and with Joseph Stalin he maintained a productive, though wary, alliance.

Ironically, the military defeat of Germany foreshadowed the political defeat of Churchill. The British people, tired of war and seeking a change, voted his party out of office in 1945. Relegated once more to a minor political role, Churchill pursued writing and a new-found interest in breeding racehorses. Both were successful. His horses won several races and his six-volume epic, *The Second World War,* was awarded a Nobel Prize in literature. His postwar years also saw him sound the alarm against Russian domination of Europe in his famous "Iron Curtain" speech at Westminster College in Missouri. Returned to power once more in 1951, his final role as Prime Minister lacked the force of his earlier one. Old age, coupled with years of brandy drinking and cigar smoking, finally took their toll.

A stroke slowed him down even more, and after the celebration of his 80th birthday in 1954, Churchill retired to Chartwell where he spent his remaining years painting, writing and savoring the great moments of history he helped create. Following his death on January 24, 1965, he was buried near his birthplace of Blenheim Palace. It is said he refused the honor of burial in Westminster Abbey since he did not wish to share eternity with so many people he did not like.

Harold "Red" Grange

"Often an All-American is made by a long run, a weak defense and an inspired writer." For some athletes perhaps. But Illinois football coach Robert Zuppke's views could not have been further from the truth when referring to the greatest halfback he ever coached, Harold "Red" Grange. Like a freight train he roared out of the Illinois cornfields and whistle-stopped to enough records to become a charter member of the Pro Football Hall of Fame. Few who saw him could forget the broken-field running style that earned Grange the nickname, "The Galloping Ghost."

Grange was born June 13, 1903, in the small Pennsylvania hamlet of Forksville. Several years later his family moved to Wheaton, Illinois, where his father, Lyle, became police chief. As a youth, Grange showed phenomenal athletic ability. By the time he finished high school, he had earned 16 letters in football, track, baseball and basketball. The facilities he used were far from elaborate. The Wheaton High School field, for instance, was located in an apple orchard and windfall apples squirted juice into the eyes of tackled players. Grange supplemented his football training by hauling 75-pound blocks of ice for a local iceman, a job which earned him thirty seven dollars a week.

Upon graduation, Grange went to the University of Illinois without being offered any type of sports scholarship. He was trying out for the seventh-string freshman squad when his bursts of speed and swift cutbacks caught the eye of an assistant coach. Head coach Robert Zuppke came to see the freshman for himself, and from that point on, Grange no longer played on the seventh-string.

His college career at Illinois was spectacular. Starting as a sophomore in 1923, he was a three-time All-American. Grantland Rice, dean of American sportswriters, wrote of him:

A streak of fire, a breath of flame,
Eluding all who reach and clutch,
A gray ghost thrown into the game
That rival hands may never touch.
A rubber bounding, blasting soul,
Whose destination is the goal—
Red Grange of Illinois.

More than 85,000 people turned out to see what was thought to be his final football game against Ohio State, in which he gained 235 yards and intercepted a pass to lead the Illini to a 14-9 victory.

But was it really his last game? During the closing weeks of his college career the sports world was swept by the rumor that Red Grange would turn professional. Sportswriters claimed this would desecrate the college game, for in 1925, professional football in no way resembled the well-oiled sports machine it is today. Its 20 teams were struggling in a haphazard, bush-league fashion that few took seriously.

A visionary Chicago promoter named Charles C. ("Cash and Carry") Pyle had dreams of changing that situation. Realizing Grange's tremendous box office appeal, Charley Pyle wanted to sign him to a one hundred thousand dollar barnstorming tour with the Chicago Bears. The presure was heavy on him not to sign, but his desire to play football was too strong. Following the Ohio State game, Grange announced his decision to quit school and play with the Chicago Bears.

What followed was an 18-day, 10-game tour that forever changed the game of professional football. Pro-attendance records were broken and Grange's name became a virtual household word. In all households, that is except one—the White House. Grange and George Halas were introduced to President Calvin Coolidge as members of the Chicago Bears, to which the President replied, "Glad to meet you young gentlemen. I always did like animal acts."

Grange was one of the first sports players to capitalize on his name through endorsements for candybars, shoes and fountain pens. He also starred in two movies, *One Minute to Play* (1926) and *Racing Romeo* (1927).

Following the barnstorming tour, Grange continued playing football, both with the Bears and briefly in a short-lived new league that Grange and Pyle founded. A knee injury in 1927 disabled him for two years, but he returned to play several more distinguished seasons. His last game was against the New York Giants in January, 1935. After being tackled on a 50-yard run, Grange knew his time was over. "When you're in the open and they catch up with you," he said sadly, "then it's time to hang up your cleats."

Grange continued to serve as assistant coach under Halas for three seasons, then entered the business world. He met Margaret Hazelburg in the fall of 1940, and the two were married in 1941. In ensuing years, Grange became a radio and television sports commentator, and in 1978, he was chosen to toss the coin for Superbowl XII at the Louisianna Superdome.

During his football career, many awards had come his way, but perhaps none more meaningful than the tribute paid by his college coach. "Red Grange," Zuppke said, "was just about as easy a man to handle as I have ever known in my coaching years. When he climbed to stardom and became the most talked about halfback in the United States, it never affected him. Conceit was foreign to his makeup. He was always modest, quiet and unassuming."

The Spider's Web

Robert Bruce was lying on a sodden, straw mattress contemplating his sorry state of affairs. He was a King without a country, a General without an army. Because of his rash belief that he could free Scotland from English domination, Scotland now lay in the grip of a conquering English army. His brother had been tortured to death, his wife taken prisoner, and many of his loyal followers were hung from the gallows as traitors.

Bruce himself barely escaped with his life to an island off the Irish coastline. The only realm over which he now presided was the miserable hut in which he dwelt. He ran his fingers through his bushy red hair and contemplated the inevitable—surrender. He had no right to subject his men to further suffering, and the dream of a free Scotland appeared hopeless. As he lay on the bed, deciding what he should do, Bruce noticed a spider hanging at the end of a long thread. It was trying to swing from one beam of the roof to another to anchor a thread and complete its web. Six times the spider failed to reach the beam, and Bruce suddenly realized that he, too, had failed six times in fighting the English. "If the spider succeeds on the next try," he thought, "so will I." Swinging in an ever greater arc, the spider exerted all its strength and landed on the far beam. Bruce took heart from this omen and once again mustered an army to battle the English. Although he had never before gained a victory, he never afterward sustained a defeat. In 1314, the last of the English armies retreated from Scotland and Robert Bruce proudly donned the robes of royalty—robes that were in a large part spun by a tiny, persevering spider.

5

Still More Redheads

Every shade of colour they were—straw, lemon, orange, brick, Irish-setter, clay; but, as Spaulding said there were not many who had the real vivid flame-coloured tint.

A.C. Doyle, *The Red-Headed League*

WILLIAM THE CONQUEROR (1035-87) In 1066, an army of 7,000 men led by William, Duke of Normandy, defeated King Harold of England at the Battle of Hastings, and thus succeeded in becoming the last foreign army to fight on English soil. A firm ruler and a strong military leader, William introduced feudalism to England and helped to organize reforms in its church system.

TYCHO BRAHE (1546-1601) Danish astronomer Tycho Brahe's precise celestial measurements led to the discovery of the laws of planetary motion. At the age of 26, he observed a supernova in the constellation Cassiopeia and verified it as a new star in the supposedly unchanging heavens. This revolutionary find, plus 20 years of work in recording planetary motion, made him one of the key figures in the formation of modern astronomy.

HENRY VIII (1491-1546) A roilsome, feisty fellow who left for posterity the Church of England and six wives who constantly turn up in trivia contests, Henry VIII made the Monarchy the visual symbol of the English nation, a symbol his daughter, Queen Elizabeth I, would raise to even loftier heights. Henry broke with the Catholic Church because of a divorce he sought from Catherine of Aragon (daughter of fellow redhead Queen Isabella). The key issue was not so much the divorce, but whether the papal commission hearing the matter should meet in Italy or England. When the Pope insisted on the former, Henry considered it an affront to English sovereignty and confiscated church property and monasteries for the Crown. One of his most influential advisors, Sir Thomas More, refused to go along with this action and was beheaded for treason. For trivia buffs, his six wives, in order, were Catherine of Aragon, Anne Boleyn, Jane Seymour, Anne of Cleves, Catherine Howard and Catherine Parr.

TITIAN (1488-1576) One of the supremely great painters of all time, Titian chose redheads, naturally enough, as the models for his portraits. His other works included religious and mythological motifs that were important influences on the Italian Renaissance.

ANTONIO VIVALDI (1678-1741) He was the composer of nearly 850 musical works that included operas, vocal music and instrumental arragements. Ordained as a priest in 1703, he acquired as a nickname "Jo Prete Russo" (the Red Priest) because of his red hair.

HARRISON GREY OTIS (1765-1848) A noted orator and early American political leader, Otis served as a U.S. Senator from 1817 to 1822, resigning that office to become the first elected mayor of Boston.

MARTIN VAN BUREN (1782-1862) Known as the "Red Fox of Kinderhook," because of his red hair and New York origins, Martin Van Buren served as the eighth President of the United States from 1836 to 1840. Van Buren was a staunch supporter of Jacksonian democracy, and he fought against slavery and the Bank of the United States, which he felt served the vested business interests of the country instead of the people as a whole. Because of his refined taste, Van Buren lost the election of 1840 to William Henry Harrison, who in a masterful promotion campaign, was portrayed as a man of the people from humble log cabin origins. It was the first election in which campaign songs played an important role. One barroom favorite went:

> Old Tip he wears a homespun suit
> He has no ruffled shirt.
> But Mat he has the golden plate
> And he's a little squirt.

GEORGE BERNARD SHAW (1856-1950) In the course of his remarkably long and productive life, Shaw was one of the most influential figures of modern literature. By the time his career got off the ground, he was nearly 40, and a confirmed vegetarian, socialist and eccentric. His earliest professional writing consisted of music and theatre reviews in which he mercilessly attacked the complacent British theatre, especially the reverence for Shakespeare, which he termed "Bardolatry." Challenged to produce better, Shaw began in 1892 to write plays that dealt with an individual's approach to social problems. This clash of wills and ideas was most apparent in plays such as *Major Barbera* (1905), which pitted an idealistic Salvation Army leader against her father who owned a munitions factory. His most popular play, *Pygmalion* (1913), was first turned into a movie in 1938, and in 1956, it was adapted into the Oscar-winning musical, *My Fair Lady.* When he died, theatres around the world were darkened in his honor.

ROBERT INGERSOLL (1833-1899) Known as the "American Demosthenes," Ingersoll traveled the length and breadth of the country to deliver lectures lambasting orthodox religions. His fiery speeches helped to loosen and expand American intellectual thought in the late 19th century. Of his personal views on life, Ingersoll once explained, "I have a creed: one, happiness is the only good; two, the way to be happy is to make others so; three, the place to be happy is here; four, the time to be happy is now."

SOLOMON SCHECHTER (1847-1915) A rabbi and scholar, Solomon Schecter was the highly esteemed president of teh Jewish Theological Seminary of America from 1902 until his death. Prior to filling this position, Schecter, in 1896, discovered the ancient archives of a Cairo synagogue. Among the ninety thousand manuscripts was a copy of the original Hebrew version of *Ecclesiasticus.* This was the most important breakthrough in Biblical research until the Dead Sea Scrolls were recovered 50 years later. As director of the Seminary, Schecter did much to structure conservative Jewish thought along traditional interpretation of the Bible.

SINCLAIR LEWIS (1885-1951) The great satirizer of the American Dream gone sour, Sinclair Lewis was the first American to win the Nobel Prize in Literature. His five important novels, *Main Street, Babbitt, Arrowsmith, Elmer Gantry* and *Dodsworth* were major attacks on the hypocrisy, conformity and commercialism that Lewis felt were rampant in the country. Alcoholism and two failed-marriages made him a lonely, unhappy man in his later life, especially since he saw no improvement in the conditions about which he wrote.

LELA SECOR (1887-1966) Not all redheads are warriors. Lela Secor was a journalist and active feminist when she sailed on the Ford Peace Expedition to Europe in 1915. Although the mission failed, it embarked her on a lifelong commitment to personal pacificism and world peace that included work with the American Neutral Conference Committee and the Emergency Peace Federation.

KATHARINE HEPBURN (1909-) The "First Lady of the American Cinema" is the only person to have won four Oscars for her acting ability—*Morning Glory* (1933), *Guess Who's Coming to Dinner* (1967), *The Lion in Winter* (1968) and *On Golden Pond* (1982). Due to poor grades in chemistry, she abandoned her plans to become a doctor and studied acting instead. After initial reviews which drily observed that she registered "the gamut of emotions, from A to B," she catapulted to fame with *The Philadelphia Story* in 1940. Two years later she starred with fellow-redhead Spencer Tracy in *Woman of the Year,* a film about a sophisticated woman columnist and an earthy sports editor. The Tracy-Hepburn chemistry worked its magic in a series of hit movies spanning 25 years, and sadly ended after the death of her close friend and co-star following the filming of *Guess Who's Coming to Dinner*. By her own admission, Katharine Hepburn is "tall, skinny and very determined."

SPENCER TRACY (1900-1967) It's hard to determine on which side of the screen Spencer Tracy delivered his best lines. As an actor, he won back-to-back Oscars for his portrayal of the Portugese fisherman in *Captains Courageous* (1937) and as Father Flanagan in *Boys Town* (1938). Off screen, when asked what advice he would give an actor who is starting his career, Tracy replied, "Learn your lines." Of Hollywood's interest in politics, he scoffed, "Before you ask more actors to get into politics, just remember who shot Lincoln." Tracy began his acting career on the New York stage, then moved to Hollywood in 1930, where he first starred at 20th Century Fox and then at M-G-M. It was at M-G-M that he began acting with Katharine Hepburn in what surely was one of the great match-ups of movie history. Tracy took his acting seriously and maintaned his appeal as a star in over 60 movies. He created for his audiences the unforgettable image of a tough individualist with a tender heart.

JOHN GLENN (1921-) The right stuff wasn't enough stuff for John Glenn during the 1984 Presidential campaign. As a middle-of-the-road Democratic candidate, Glenn was predicted to pose a formidable challenge, but his primary campaign fell apart because of a lack of focus. In the early 1960s, however, there was one race he did help win - the space race. On February 20, 1962, John Glenn blasted off in the Mercury space capsule *Friendship 7* to become the first American to orbit the earth. More than any of the other early astronauts, Glenn seemed to embody the spirit of adventure in the "New Frontiers" of President John F. Kennedy. New York accorded him the largest tickertape parade in its history. Throughout most of his political career, Glenn lamented that the question most people wanted to discuss with him was "Do astronauts drink Tang?"

STEVE ROPER & MIKE NOMAD BY SAUNDERS & MATERA

By permission of the News America Syndicate

SONNY JURGENSEN (1934-) The "Flingin Redhead" was the heart and soul of the Washington Redskins during the 1960s and the early 1970s. One of the best passing quarterbacks in the game, Jurgensen led his "Over-the-Hill-Gang" of veteran pros against the Miami Dolphins in the 1973 Superbowl. The Redskins lost 14-7, and in 1975 Jurgensen retired after 18 years of professional football. He is now a sports commentator for a Washington television station.

Some Redheaded "Reds"

Arnold Jacob "Red" Auerbach, president and former coach of the Boston Celtics
Richard "Red" Skelton, actor and comedian
"Red" Grooms, contemporary American artist
Albert Fred "Red" Schoendist, former player and coach of the St. Louis Cardinals
Walter Lanier "Red" Barber, former baseball sportscaster
Paul Neal "Red" Adair, oil well troubleshooter
Walter Wellesley "Red" Smith, former sports columnist, died in 1982
Morris "Red" Badgro, enshrined in Football Hall of Fame

LITTLE ORPHAN ANNIE (1924-) Leapin Lizards! Is she that old? The little redhead has been shining her blank peepers at us for over six decades. Annie first appeared as a comic strip in the New York *News* on August 5, 1924, and from there she has gone on to star in radio, Broadway and television. Perhaps no strip has ever maintained such a fine sense of adventure interspersed with street-wise tough-talk. Her creator, Harold Gray, who died in 1968, kept the strip simple—good guys vs. bad guys with the former winning out. Annie always maintained a ladylike sense of decency and honor, but was never afraid to mix it up with bullies. One classic exchange read, "Sock me, will yuh? Yuh big yap—Play THAT one on yer piccolo."

LUCILLE BALL (1911-) The "Crazy Redhead" of television and movies has been delighting viewers with her wacky humor for over 30 years. When *I Love Lucy* first appeared in 1951, little did she know that the series, along with two subsequent ones (*The Lucy Show* and *Here's Lucy*), would accumulate scores of honors and eventually appear in 77 countries. With Fred and Ethel Murtz, Ricy Ricardo and Little Ricky, she became a part of the American Way of Life. Not only a gifted actress, Lucille Ball is also a shrewd businesswoman who successfully managed Desilu Productions from 1962 to 1967, and Lucille Ball Productions from 1968. Among her countless awards were the "Lucy Day" at the New York World's Fair in 1964, and the designation, "Comedienne of the Century." It's a fitting triumph for a woman who was a 15-year-old washout at the John Murray Anderson-Robert Milton Dramatic School in New York City.

MAUREEN O'HARA (1921-) Described as having the "perfect Technicolor complexion," Maureen O'Hara was one of Hollywood's leading stars of the 1940s. The Irish-born actress grew up near Dublin and began her acting career at the famous Abbey Theatre. She came to the United States in 1939 and starred in such classics as *How Green was My Valley* (1941), *Miracle of 34th Street* (1946), and that unforgettable epic of cinematography, *The Redhead from Wyoming* (1952).

MALCOLM X (1925-1965) Born Malcolm Little, nicknamed Detroit Red and named Malcolm X, this charismatic black leader was an important figure in the expansion of black awareness during the 1960s. After his father was killed in Michigan by white racists, he moved to Manhattan where he survived as a hustler, numbers runner and burglar. At one point he worked as a waiter in a Harlem restaurant with Chicago Red - Redd Foxx. After a burglary conviction, Malcolm X used his time in prison to study and read. Attracted to the teachings of Elijah Muhammad, he became a Black Muslim and served as its leading spokesman after his release from jail. Later his doubts about this version of Islam caused him to break with the Black Muslims and start his own Organization of African-American Unity. His articulate expounding of painful truths earned him wide respect in the black community. Malcolm X was assasinated in Harlem in 1965 Before his death, however, he collaborated with Alex Haley on a book that has become a classic - *The Autobiography of Malcolm X.*

DANNY KAYE (1913-) Danny Kaye, through his hilarious comedy and humanitarian efforts, has earned a well-deserved place in the world's heart. Born in Brooklyn, Kaye abandoned his dream of becoming a surgeon and left high school to become an entertainer. After several summers on the Borscht Circuit in the Catskills, Kaye joined a vaudeville troop in 1933 and toured the United States and the Orient. Returning to the United States in 1936, Kaye booked several new comedy roles. With the help of pianist-composer Sylvia Fine, whom he married in 1940, Kaye perfected his famous double-talk comic delivery. His career blossomed in Hollywood, where he displayed his talents in such multiple-role movies as *The Secret Life of*

Walter Mitty (1947), and *The Inspector General* (1949). In recent years, Kaye has devoted his attention to the Seattle Mariners baseball team, of which he is an owner. He still has time, however, for performing in a role that is dear to his heart—permanent ambassador-at-large for UNICEF.

BEVERLY SILLS (1929-) The folks in Brooklyn thought "Bubbles" Silverman had done it all when at the age of three she starred in radio's "Uncle Bob's Rainbow Hour." Years later Bubbles, now known as Beverly Sills, would go on to become one of the finest opera singers in the world. Retiring from the stage in 1980, she is currently the general director of the New York City Opera.

RODNEY LAVER (1938-) Nicknamed "the Rocket" because of his powerful left-handed service, Laver dominated amateur and professional tennis during the 1960s and early 1970s. He grew up on a ranch in the Australian bush country, and was introduced to the sport on a court made out of flattened anthills. From there he went on to win four Wimbledon singles titles and two grand-slams of the Australian, French, British and American championships. Laver was the first tennis player to earn over a million dollars at the game, but even more importantly, the tennis world will remember him as being one of its last bastions of sportsmanlike, professional conduct.

TOM ROBBINS (1936-) A widely popular fiction writer, Tom Robbins' novels flow from insanely imaginative settings that include baboons, goat ranches and the mummified body of Jesus Christ. His third novel, *Still Life with Woodpecker,* contains, among other things, a recipe list for homemade bombs. It is must reading for connoisseurs of redhead-literature, since it cogently argues that the design on a Camel cigarette pack is a message from redheads on the planet Argon. Robbins once told an interviewer, "No other animal has a sense of humor, the highest wisdom in the world. And we're the only animal that falls in love. The absurd extent to which human beings go when they're in love justifies their existence."

WOODY ALLEN (1935-) Is Woody Allen a neurotic genius or a genius at being neurotic? Filmgoers are still trying to figure out the answer to that question. An Oscar-winning director (*Annie Hall,* 1977), Allen has developed a wide following for his films which range from wacky humor to bittersweet romance. A short man with auburn hair, Allen's film roles in such movies as *Play It Again, Sam* (1972) are spoofs of a neurotic, less than macho guy trying to become a conquering lover.

Allen was born in Brooklyn and grew up as a lonely kid who mostly read comic books. But his writing talent became apparent at an early age. While still in high school, he began supplying one-liners for comics, a talent that landed him a job on television's *Garry Moore Show.*

Leaving that job in 1961, Allen developed his own stand-up comic routine. Three years later Allen wrote the screen play to *What's New Pussycat* (1965). Unhappy with losing artistic control over the movie, Allen decided to both write and direct his own films, and he has turned out a string of box office successes.

SARAH FERGUSON (1960-) "Fergie" to her friends, princess to the rest of us, this lovely British lass joins the royal family as the bride of Prince Andrew. One can only wonder how many "hairs" to the throne the couple may have.

Group Dynamics

Those people who think there is a club for everything are absolutely correct. For redheads, two organizations that exist are Redheads International, 23101 Moulton Parkway, Suite 110 Laguna Hills, CA 92653 and Flaming Locks, c/o Frederick Holl, P.O. Box 22365, Seattle WA 98122.

The Artistic Redhead

Q—What did Arthur Conan Doyle, Zane Grey and William Butler Yeats have in common?

A—They all wore argyle socks and wrote about redheads.

Redheads really have a way of shining out in art and literature. All of the above writers composed works that featured redheads. Yeats' poetry had a character, Red Hanrahan, who was the narrator of "Red Hanrahan's Song About Ireland." Doyle schemed up a nefarious plot involving the establishment of a curious Redheaded League as the front to cover a bank robbery. Only Sherlock Holmes could pierce through the scheme and bring the bounders to justice. Zane Grey had a little less ambition, and ignored writing about an entire league in favor of simply focusing on *The Redheaded Outfield.*

In the movies and in art, redheads stand out like million-watt beacons. The play *Annie,* after appearing for years on Broadway, was a huge success as Aileen Quinn danced her way across the screen. Cindy Lauper has picked up the torch and has carried the persona to new, well, different heights in showing that redheads just want to have fun. Painters have always appreciated the way a redhead can rivet attention to a scene on canvas. Titian, James Whistler, Charles Peale and Red Grooms are artists who have successfully used redheads as models. One anonymous painter summed it up when he observed, "You can mix any color with some other color and get a different one except when you mix red hair."

Afterwords

There are two phrases most dear to the heart of an author—"Chapter One," and "The End." For you who have been my most appreciated audience, please view this book as merely a step towards a new beginning. If it has helped to inspire you, or bring new depths to your self-awareness, then use this powerful knowledge as a tool in assisting others for their growth. The world today is facing a massive energy shortage that has nothing to do with oil and gas. For it is an energy shortage of the spirit. As fear over war, unemployment, pollution and a score of other evils sap mankind's strength, a gray fog of despair is enveloping the planet. Now is the time for redheads, and all other men and women of courage and stout heart to pierce through this miasma as guiding lights of resolute vitality. This is our greatest challenge. Indeed, it is our greatest obligation.

Sources

Chapter 1

Allen, Arthur. *The Skin, A Clinopathologic Treatise.* The C.V. Mosley Co., St. Louis, 1954.

Barnicot, N.A. "Red Hair in African Negroes: A Preliminary Study," *Annals of Eugenics,* 17, (1953), 211-21.

—"The Pigment Trichosiderin, from Human Red Hair," *Nature,* 177, (1956, 528-9.

—"The Relation of the Pigment Trichosiderin to Hair Colour," *Annals of Human Genetics,* 21, (1956), 31-9.

Birbeck, M. "The Structure and Formation of Pigment Granules in Human Hair," *Experimental Cell Research,* 10 (1956), 505-14.

Brown, Dr. Algie C., ed. *The First Human Hair Symposium.* Medcom Press, New York, 1974.

Edison, Thomas. *The Diary of Thomas Edison.* Chatham Press, Old Greenwood, Conn., 1962.

Flesch, Peter, Rothman, Stephen. "Isolation of an Iron Pigment from Human Red Hair," *Journal of Investigative Dermatology,* 6 (1945), 257-70.

Goodman, Dr. Herman. *Your Hair.* Halcyon House, Garden City, New York, 1943.

Harsanyi, Z.P., Brinkman, Jeannie, Post, P.W. "Mutagenicity of Melanin from Human Red Hair," *Experientia,* (1980), 291-2.

Kobori, Tatsuji, Montagna, William. *Biology and Diseases of the Hair.* University of Tokyo Press, Tokyo, 1976.

Montagna, William, Ellis, Richard. *The Biology of Hair Growth.* Academic Press, New York, 1958.

Reed, T.E. "Red Hair Colour as a Genetical Character," *Annals of Eugenics,* 17, (1952), 115-39.

Rook, Arthur, Wilkinson, D.S., Ebling, F.J. *The Textbook of Dermatology.* Blackwell Scientific Pub., London, 1975.

Saller, K., Martin, R. *Lehrbuch der Anthropologie.* Gustav Fischer Verlag, Stuttgart, 3rd edition, Vol. 3, 1962.

Singh, Kirpal. *The Sikh Symbols.* Sikh Missionary Society, Kent, England, 1971.

Singleton, W. Ralph, Ellis, Brenda. "Inheritance of Red Hair for Six Generations," *The Journal of Heredity,* 55 (1964), 261.

Reader's Digest Assn. *Strange Stories, Amazing Facts.* Pleasantville, N.Y., 1976

Chapter 2

Bar, Michael, Wintner, Yitzhak, Davidson, Shamai. "Hyperactive Behavior in Redheaded Children," *Eugenics Society Bulletin,* 12(1980), 48-52.

Barkley, Russell A. *Hyperactive Children,* The Guilford Press, New York, 1981.

Boucher, Alan. *Sea Kings and Dragon Ships.* Walker and Co., New York, 1964.

Boulnois, Luce, *The Silk Route.* E.P. Dutton, New York, 1966.

Cantwell, Dr. Dennis P. "The 'Hyperactive' Child," *Hospital Practice,* (Jan. 1979), 65-73.

Graham-Campbell, James. *The Viking World.* Ticknor and Fields, New York, 1980.

Kirby, Michael. *The Vikings.* E.P. Dutton, New York, 1977.

Harper, H.A., Rodwell, V.W., Mayes, P.A. *Review of Physiological Chemistry.* Lange Medical Publications, Los Altos, Calif., 16th edition, 1977.

Lester, David. *A Physiological Basis for Personality Traits.* Charles C. Thomas, Springfield, Ill., 1974.

McGovern, William Montgomery. *The Early Empires of Central Asia.* UNC Press, Chapel Hill, N.C., 1939.

Ross, Dorothea, Ross, Sheila. *Hyperactivity: Research, Theory and Action.* John Wiley and Sons, New York, 1976.

Smith, Dr. Lendon. *Improving Your Child's Behavior Chemistry.* Prentice-Hall, Inc., New Jersey, 1976.

Wender, Dr. Paul. *The Hyperactive Child.* Crown Publishers, New York, 1973.

Chapter 3

Bonwick, James. *Irish Druids and Old Irish Religions.* Griffith Farrin and Co., London, 1894.

Bunce, John Thackeray. *Fairy Tales, Their Origin and Meaning.* MacMillan and Co., London, 1878.

Clark, Rundle. *Myth and Symbol in Ancient Egypt.* Grove Press, New York, 1960.

Budge, Wallis. *Osiris, The Egyptian Religion of Resurrection.* University Books, New York, 1961.

Bullfinch, Thomas. *Bullfinch's Mythology.* Thomas Y. Crowell Co., New York, 1947.

Frazer, Sir James. *The Golden Bough.* MacMillan and Co., London, 1922.

Hull, Eleanor. *Cuchulain, The Hound of Ulster.* George G. Harrup and Co., 1911.
—*The Cuchulain Saga in Irish Literature,* David Nutt in the Strand, London, 1898.
Ivens, Walter G. *The Island Builders of the South Pacific,* Seely, Service and Co., London, 1930.
Jubainville, H. *The Irish Mythological Cycle.* Hodges Figgis and Co., Dublin, 1903.
Little Red Riding Hood and Other Fairy Tales. Penn Publishing Co., Philadelphia, 1918.
Little Red Riding Hood. Rand McNally and Co., Chicago, 1933.
Machowski, Jacek. *Island of Secrets.* Robert Hale, London, 1969.
Maziere, Francis. *Mysteries of Easter Island* Collins, London, 1969.
Mercante, Anthony. *Who's Who in Egyptian Religion,* Clarkson N. Potter, Inc., New York, 1978.
Ogott, Bethwell. "British Administration in the Central Nyanza District of Kenya 1900-60," *Journal of African History,* 2 (1963), 249-73.
Olcott, William. *Sun Lore of All Ages.* Putnam, New York, 1914.
Palmer, A. Smythe. *The Samson Saga.* Sir Isaac Pitman and Sons, Ltd., 1903.
Routeledge, Katherine. *The Mystery of Easter Island.* Hazell, Watson and Viney, London, 1919.
Tanner, Florice. *Mystery Teachings in World Religions.* Theosophical Publishing House, Wheaton, Ill., 1973.
Titcomb, Sarah E. *Aryan Sun Myths, The Origin of Religions.* Nims and Knight, Troy, N.Y., 1889.
Thompson, C.J.S. *The Hand of Destiny.* Rider and Co., London, 1932.
Westermarck, Edward. *Pagan Survivals in Mohammedan Civilization,* Macmillan and Company, London, 1933
Wolff, Werner, *Island of Death,* Hacker Art Books, New York, 1973.

Chapter 4

Owens, Clifford. P., ed. *A Story of Jesus, Based on the Edgar Cayce Readings.* A.R.E. Press, Virginia Beach, Va., 1963.
Ludwig, Emil. *Cleopatra, the Story of a Queen.* Gallen and Unwin, Ltd., London, 1938.
Lindsay, Jack. *Cleopatra.* Constable, London, 1971.
Franzero, Charles. *The Life and Times of Cleopatra.* Heron Books, London, 1968.

Ingstad, Helge. *Westward to Vinland.* St. Martin's Press, New New York, 1969.
Pohl, Frederick. *The Viking Explorers.* Thomas Y. Crowell Co., New York, 1966.
Smith, Charles. *Northmen of Adventure.* Longmans, Green and Co., New York, 1932.

Fernandez-Armesto, Felipe. *Ferdinand and Isabella.* Weidenfield and Nicolson, London, 1975.
McKendrick, Melvina. *Ferdinand and Isabella.* Harper and Row, New York, 1968.
Plunkett, Irene. *Isabelle of Castille and the Making of the Spanish Nation.* G.P. Putnam's Sons, New York, 1915.

Morison, Samuel Eliot. *Admiral of the Ocean Sea.* Little, Brown and Co., Boston, 1942.
Sargent, Daniel, *Christopher Columbus.* Bruce Publishing, Milwaukee, 1941.

Jenkins, Elizabeth. *Elizabeth the Great.* Coward-McCann, New York, 1959.
Levine, Joseph, *Elizabeth I,* Prentice Hall, New Jersey, 1969.
Maynard, Theodore, *Queen Elizabeth,* Bruce Publishing Co., Milwaukee, 1954.

Fleming, Thomas. *First in Their Hearts.* W.W. Norton and Co., New York, 1968.
Robert Jones. *George Washington.* Twayne Publishers, Boston, 1979.
Eichner, James. *Thomas Jefferson, the Complete Man,* Franklin Watts, New York, 1966.
Johnston, Johanna. *Thomas Jefferson, His Many Talents.* Dodd, Mead and Co., New York, 1961.
Wibberly, Leonard. *Man of Liberty, A Life of Thomas Jefferson,* Farrar, Strauss and Giroux, New York, 1968.
Johnson, Gerald W., *The First Captain, The Story of John Paul Jones.* Coward-McCann Inc., New York, 1947.
Russell, Phillips. *John Paul Jones, Man of Action.* Brentano's, New York, 1927.
DeLaCroix, Robert. *John Paul Jones.* Frederick Muller Ltd., London, 1960.
Higgins, David. *Portrait of Emily Dickinson.* Rutgers University Press, New Brunswick, N.J., 1967.

Johnson, Thomas. *Emily Dickinson-An Interpretive Biography.* Atheneum, New York, 1972.

Wilburn, Richard, ed. *Emily Dickinson.* Dell Publishing, New York, 1960.

Lincoln, Victoria. *A Private Disgrace, Lizzie Borden by Daylight,* Gollancy, London, 1968.

Radin, Edward D. *Lizzie Borden: the Untold Story.* Gollancy, London, 1961.

Sullivan, Robert. *Goodbye Lizzie Borden.* S. Greene Press, Brattleboro, Vt., 1974.

Elgar, Frank. *Van Gogh: A Study of his Life and Work.* Praeger, New York, 1966.

Hanson, Lawrence. *Passionate Pilgrim; the Life of Vincent Van Gogh.* New York, Random House, 1955.

Noble, Iris. *Great Lady of the Theatre.* Julian Messner, Inc., New York, 1960.

Skinner, Cornelia. *Madame Sarah.* Houghton Mifflin, Boston 1967.

Verneuil, Louis. *The Fabulous Life of Sarah Bernhardt.* Harper and Brothers, New York, 1942.

Lader, Lawrence, Meltzer, Milton. *Margaret Sanger, Pioneer of Birth Control.* Thomas Y. Crowell Co., New York, 1969.

Lorgney, Virginia. Margaret Sanger, Rebel With A Cause, Doubleday and Co., Inc., Garden City, N.Y., 1969.

Werner, Vivian. *Margaret Sanger: Woman Rebel.* Hawthorne Books, New York, 1970.

Charnock, Joan. *Red Revolutionary, a Life of Lenin.* Hawthorne Books, New York, 1970.

Pearson, Michael. *The Sealed Train.* G.P. Putnam's Sons, New York, 1975.

Albjerg, Victor. *Winston Churchill.* Twayne Publishers, New York, 1973.

Bocci, Geoffrey. *The Adventurous Life of Winston Churchill.* Julian Messner, Inc., New York, 1958.

Grange, Harold Edward. *The Red Grange Story, the Autobiography of Red Grange, as told to Ira Norton,* Putnam, New York, 1953.

Wiesbusch, John. *Red Grange.* NFL Properties, Canton, Ohio, 1978.

Index